THE COLOR PURPLE

A Memory Book of The Broadway Musical

Text and Interviews by Lise Funderburg

Principal Photography by Jennifer S. Altman

With Production Photography by Paul Kolnik

Designed by 3+Co.

To Alice Walker and her ancestors, whose voices started it all and who continue to watch over us.

Published by

CARROLL & GRAF

Produced by

MELCHER MEDIA

THE COLOR PURPLE

A Memory Book of the Broadway Musical

Published by
Carroll & Graf Publishers
An Imprint of the Avalon Publishing Group, Inc.

245 West 17th St., 11th Floor
New York, NY 10011

Produced by

124 West 13th Street
New York, NY 10011
www.melcher.com

Text by Lise Funderburg
Principal Photography by Jennifer Altman
Production Photography by Paul Kolnik
Design by 3+Co. www.threeandco.com
Editorial Consultant: Carol Fineman

Music and lyrics of *The Color Purple* by
Brenda Russell, Allee Willis, and Stephen Bray
Book of *The Color Purple* by Marsha Norman
Based upon the novel written by Alice Walker
and the Warner Bros./Amblin Entertainment Motion Picture

The Color Purple libretto is reproduced here as an abridged version.

Acknowledgments, additional copyright information,
photography and other credits, constituting an
extension of the copyright page, appear on page 184.

Library of Congress Cataloging-in-Publication Data is available.

10 9 8 7 6 5 4 3 2 1

ISBN-13: 978-0-78671-844-3
ISBN-10: 0-7867-1844-7

The Table of Contents

FOREWORD BY

I first read Alice Walker's novel *The Color Purple* more than twenty years ago, and I immediately understood it would be a powerful, ongoing force in my life. As you may know, when I'm passionate about something—especially a great book—I share it with as many people as possible. Back then, I used to pass out copies of the novel to friends and strangers with the hope that they'd read it and experience what had touched me so deeply. Courage, redemption, love, and hope—I learned so much from this story!

Nearly two years after I discovered the book, Quincy Jones and Steven Spielberg gave me the opportunity to play the role of Sofia in the feature film version. That turned out to be not only my big screen debut, but also one of the greatest experiences of my life.

Twenty years later, I'm blessed to be a part of the team presenting *The Color Purple* on the Broadway stage—it's a full-circle moment in my life.

The first day I met the cast of the Broadway musical, I told them that purple is a divine color, and it's true. What's astounding to me is how unique each new version of *The Color Purple* has been, and how true and powerful to the original they all are. With the musical, everyone on the stage, behind the scenes, and in the audience experiences and bares witness to something extraordinarily transcendent and uplifting.

Much of that credit is due to the spirit of our ancestors that lives on within the heart of Alice Walker's original story, and also to the hard work, creativity, and incredible commitment to excellence and authenticity that has been captured in this memory book.

It makes me so very proud to know that *The Color Purple* will reach a new generation of audiences. I invite you to share the experience with the hope that it will become a powerful force in your life as well.

Blessings,
Oprah Winfrey

Chapter One

The Journey

When producer Scott Sanders first hatched the notion of turning The Color Purple *into a Broadway show, naysayers had a field day. Sure, the material was rich: Alice Walker's novel was without question ensconced in the American literary canon—it's a Pulitzer Prize and National Book Award winner, has sold more than five million copies, and is to this day among the top five most reread books in America. But some skeptics wondered how musical theater would treat a story arc that spanned four decades and dealt with issues of infanticide, domestic violence, racial oppression, and spiritual crisis. Others felt that Steven Spielberg's 1985 cinematic adaptation—with memorable performances by Whoopi Goldberg, Danny Glover, and Oprah Winfrey—would overshadow any other attempts at dramatization. What Scott Sanders knew—and what kept him going through the eight years it took to secure permissions, backing, and a creative team that could produce a show that honored the material—was that music is a way to express emotions that transcend words, and that the message, the heartbeat of Walker's story (much of it rooted in her own family history), sang.*

THE JOURNEY BEGINS

ALICE WALKER: When I was eight, I went to live with my grandparents in Putnam County, Georgia, for six months. They offered me that grandparently unconditional love and safety and quiet. They talked very, very little. They seemed to me to be people who had lived very full lives. They were not people who sat around ever saying, I wish I had, I coulda, shoulda, woulda. They had this sense of completion that made being with them such a joy; I knew that there was a real bottom to their existence, that they were truly in themselves, in their own bodies, in their spirits, in their souls. My grandmother went to the Hardshell Baptist Church, but she was also a midwife and a gardener, and both she and my grandfather were very much connected to growing things. And so their spirituality never struck me as being really churchy. It was more fundamental. These were people who were the farthest back that I knew in my family and it meant that I had a certain bedrock in their experience of life. And their lives had been hard. Very hard, very difficult. So that was part of what was percolating in me: Who were these people? How did they come to this balance? How did they sit there in their seventies with a real sense of having given life all that they had and life having given them all that it offered and they were fine? Now, how did this happen? We're talking about people under segregation, racial abuse, rampant sexism, and they had this pure love to give to their granddaughter.

Alice Walker

Years and years later, I was an editor in New York at *Ms.* magazine and living in an enormous limestone with my husband. We were doing well, but it was not conducive to this story I needed to tell based on this feeling of finding your connection to what is real for you and resting there. I knew I had to give it the space it required. So I moved to California, and eventually ended up in a little town called Booneville—and had a new lover, which was helpful.

I worked on the novel for a year. In great ecstasy. Writing it was an ecstatic experience—I was probably as high as I'll ever be. The thing is, when you give yourself to others, they give themselves to you. I totally gave myself to the people [in the book]. They have parts that I could glean as an eight-year-old child, but they're also these archetypal figures, and so I was very clear about serving them, putting myself in the position of absolute devotion to their realization. I understood that if I could do that, because they are archetypes, they actually had the power to heal. And this is what people are responding to. They may disagree with this or that, but the elemental truth of each archetype makes people reach for what is highest and most fully expressed in themselves. They can't avoid it.

I'm proud that people can see at last what a gift it is. It was a gift to me, and it's a gift through me to people. [Along the way] it has been fraught with those who felt attacked and defensive and upset and scared. In other words, many were unable to open to this unconditional love the novel offers. The novel is not about fighting or abusing in any way. It's about helping people see that we are just human beings here. We're really trying to live lives that are fulfilling and happy. Some of the places explored in this book are about where we get off track and go off in the absolute wrong direction. And that's not a crime. It's not a sin. It's just what happens on earth. We do that. And black people, because we've been so used to abuse for all kinds of reasons, have a fear that if we show these places where we go off the track and we do terrible things, that we'll just encourage more abuse and more misunderstanding.

And again, *The Color Purple* is basically about helping to heal people in their relationships with each other, with themselves, and with the earth, the planet. It's also to help them reconsider inherited gods. When you inherit a god, it's like inheriting anything else. It's not yours in the sense that you did not earn it, you did not create it, it is not *yours* yours. It may well be a wonderful gift. It may well be something that has helped you shape your life. It may well be something that delights you and that guides you and all of that. But it may also be something you would not have chosen. It's well worth taking a few months or weeks or however long the processes take to consider that. Just sit down and say, Hmmm, if I had my druthers, would I actually have chosen this particular religion, this particular god? Would I be Muslim? Would I be Christian? Would I be Jewish?

For African Americans it's particularly crucial that we do this. Because after all, the facts are that we did not choose Christianity. Nor did we choose Islam. These were both forced on us in brutal ways. Now, there's a lot to be said—and I often say it—for the way that we have transformed these religions. But they still leave, in my opinion, a great deal lacking because they don't really allow and permit and encourage each person to explore what is really wanted by this particular spirit.

So what I think of as my greatest gift is this possibility of re-examining inherited religion and also seeking to decolonize the spirit. We need to decolonize our spirits in the same way that we try to decolonize our thoughts. Our brains. This is a very long journey.

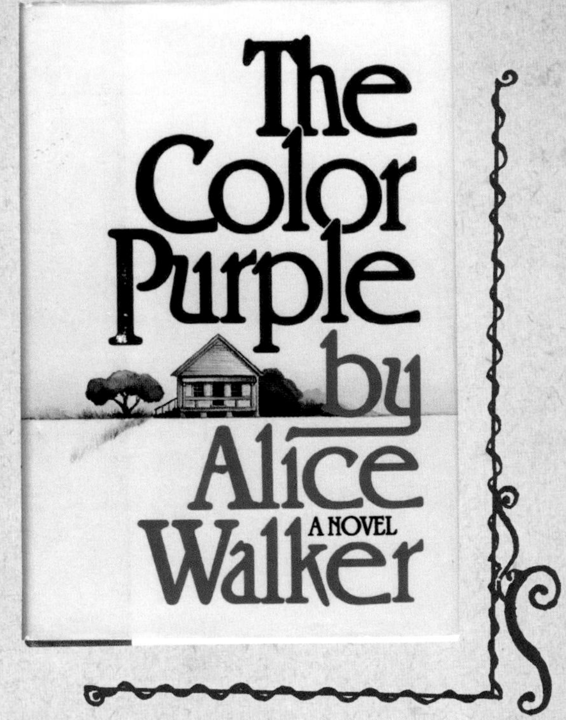

The first edition of the novel, The Color Purple, *which has sold over five million copies.*

"The Color Purple" by Alice Walker

The more I wonder, he say, the more I love.

And people start to love you back, I bet, I say.

They do, he say, surprise. Harpo love me. Sofia and the children. ~~Henrietta as big a mystery to me as a star.~~ Even ol' evil Henrietta love me a little bit. But that's cause she know she just as big a mystery to me as ~~a star~~ the moon.

Mr. ______ ~~[illegible]~~ is patterning a shirt for folks to wear wit my pants.

Got to have pockets, he say. Got to have loose sleeves. And definitely you not spose to wear it with no tie. Folks wearing ties look like they being lynch.

And then, just when I know I can live content without Shug, just when Mr. ______ ast me to marry him again, this time in the spirit as well as the ~~body~~ flesh, & just after I say Naw, ~~but let's be friends~~ I still don't like frogs, but let's us be friends, Shug write she coming home.

Now. Is this life or not?

I be so calm.

If she come, I be happy. If she don't, I be content.

Sometimes I feel mad at her. Feel like I could scratch her hair right off her head. But then I think: Shug got a right to live too. She got a right to look over the world in whatever company she choose. Just cause I love her don't take away none of her rights.

The only thing bother me is she don't never say nothing bout coming back. And I miss her. I miss her friendship so much that if she want to come back here dragging Germaine I'd make them both welcome, or die trying. Who am I to tell her who to love? My job just to love her good and true myself.

Mr. ______ ast me the other day what it is I love so much bout Shug. He say he love her style. He say to tell the truth, Shug act more manly than most men. I mean she upright, honest. Speak her mind & the devil take the hindmost, he say. You know Shug will fight, he say. Just like Sofia. She bound to live her life & be herself no matter what.

Mr. ______ think all this is stuff I tell men do. But Harpo not like this. You not like this. What Shug got is womanly it seem like to me. Specially since she & Sofia the ones got it.

Sofia and Shug not like men, he say. They not like women either.

You mean, they not like me or you.

Scott Sanders

STARTING FROM THE SHOW'S BEGINNINGS

SCOTT SANDERS (Lead Producer): *The Color Purple* moved me from the first time I read it, in the 1980s. Celie was a great protagonist, and although my life in no way mirrored hers, in the same way that every person has to overcome adversity in life and deal with obstacles and hardships, it spoke to me that she was able to pick herself up and move forward day after day. To watch her find self-love and self-respect and self-esteem even while questioning her own spiritual faith was phenomenal and inspiring.

When I started to think seriously about doing this as a musical, Celie baffled me. I couldn't understand how someone could be that positive and have to endure what she did. I understood hating Mister. I could never understand being able to forgive Mister. I understood her being angry at God. But it struck me as remarkable that Celie wasn't bitter. Someone who had her life could easily be angry at the world, but she was consistently there for others, whether it was Sofia or Harpo—who was not so nice to her when he was a kid.

Once Celie finds her sister's letters, she's able to take a drop of hope and let it wash over her. And I thought, Wow! That is so amazing, for someone to not just fall apart, not just cave in, not just lose it on some level. I used to wonder, Where did it come from? Did it come from her spiritual connection to God?

While the character in the story is an African-American female and I'm a white male, it moved me. I can't explain why I have had such a strong connection to African-American culture and music and stories. I grew up in St. Petersburg, Florida, which is not exactly the South. I did go to a mostly black high school during the mid-seventies, and so I was exposed to the culture. When I came to New York and started producing concerts at Radio City Music Hall, almost all the early shows were black artists, from Diana Ross and Marvin Gaye to the Commodores and Aretha Franklin. So it's been part of my DNA to be connected to those kinds of stories, artists, and music.

"Once Celie finds
her sister's letters
she's able to take
a drop of hope and
let it wash over her.
And I thought, Wow!"

— SCOTT SANDERS

GETTING ALICE TO SIGN ON

SCOTT SANDERS: When I went to see Alice Walker to ask for the rights, I knew that this was not just another book. I was asking for the rights to something beloved and there was going to be a tremendous amount of pressure on me to deliver. I even said to Alice early on, "I am not going to be the guy to screw this up. If there's ever a moment you feel like I am not doing this correctly, I'll stop."

I've worked with many, many artists in my life, and so I did not feel in any way intimidated about meeting Alice before I got to her house in Berkeley. Then I walked into her house, and my nerves changed.

Alice's house stood out on the street; it was painted these beautiful, bold Mexican colors. I went inside and several women were doing things in the kitchen and stuff was going on. Her house felt almost like a commune.

Alice was friendly, very friendly, and could not have been nicer. But if I was trying to figure out what she was thinking, there was no way I was going to do that. I was never going to see anything other than what she decided to show me. She is very quiet. It was a little unnerving because as a producer you meet people and try to figure out what they're saying and what they're not saying. There was no way I was going to penetrate that wall in Alice Walker.

ALICE WALKER: When Scott first came to me, I was not thrilled. I was just kind of bemused. Here is this very earnest-seeming person who I've never heard of, and he wants to make a musical. There are always people wanting to do this and that with my novels, make music out of my poems. I just didn't really respond all that enthusiastically. But he was persistent. And that was very much in his favor.

SCOTT SANDERS: First she said no. She didn't think it was a good idea, and she didn't want to revisit the story. I didn't realize that when the controversy bubbled up in the media after the movie, what a painful experience it had been for her. I didn't understand that at the time.

While I was in the house—maybe it was the presence of those other women—I said, "Well, you're a smart woman, and you obviously care about what other women think. I've had the privilege of working with some really amazing women in my career. And if you'd like to call any of them and get a reference, clearly, I'm not asking you to say yes to this before you check me out." And she said, "I would like to do that."

ALICE WALKER: I called these women that Scott recommended. Each one said, "If anybody can do it, Scott Sanders can." It felt better to have these women, like Whoopi Goldberg and Bette Midler and Diana Ross say a good word for him, because I like all of them and I respect them.

SCOTT SANDERS: Then I asked if she would come to New York and see some theater and let me talk to her more about my vision. And she did.

ALICE WALKER: I didn't live in New York anymore, and the last wonderful thing I'd seen was *Jesus Christ Superstar*. I remembered that, which was lucky. Because I thought if they can put that on Broadway then maybe I can have some hope.

SCOTT SANDERS: We saw *Bring in 'Da Noise/ Bring in 'Da Funk*. We saw *The Fantastiks*.

ALICE WALKER: Whatever we saw, I liked it. I paid a lot of attention to how well things were done. I was concerned that there would be some degree of tackiness; that would not have been possible for me to endure.

SCOTT SANDERS: To cap off the week, I wanted her to meet the entertainment community of New York so she could have a sense of where this was going to live and breathe. I decided to do a dinner party on a boat that would cruise around Manhattan. I invited a bunch of people, about fifty, from the theater world.

I said to Alice, "Feel free to ask them what they think about this. Here's a chance to do your due diligence with an industry that you don't know. This is going to be a long, tough road, and it's going to be very challenging. I don't want you doing this unless you really feel good about it."

ALICE WALKER: He pulled out every stop. It was truly luminous. Since I don't move in those circles much, I don't remember who they all were.

My friend Pratibha [Parmar] had flown over from London, and we just enjoyed it. We had a ball. But the main thing was Scott himself. I watched him very closely, and I was really impressed with him as a human being. I knew that even if we did something together and it failed, it would be perfectly fine. We would have learned wonderful things about life, and it would have been a very good journey.

SCOTT SANDERS: At the end of the New York trip she said, "I agree. And I'm ready to do this." I was so excited. I had no idea that the rights were also held by Warner Brothers and Steven Spielberg. I thought Alice's blessing would be helpful. But I didn't know Steven Spielberg, and I had no idea of whether he would think it was a good idea. Then I had to go through a two-year process with Warner Brothers and Spielberg's Amblin Entertainment to get the rights. There were many times along that path that I thought, Oh, brother, this is way too hard. But I just kept persevering, and while that was going on, I thought, Well, let me not waste this time completely. I'm going to assume that I'm going to get it, and let me start thinking about the people who could write it.

The poster for the 1985 movie, which starred Whoopi Goldberg, Oprah Winfrey, and Danny Glover.

Allee Willis, Stephen Bray, and Brenda Russell

WHO SHOULD WRITE THE SONGS?

SCOTT SANDERS: As I started to do research, I felt that it was important to have authentic voices in the writing of *The Color Purple* for the stage. While I completely understood that you didn't have to live in Georgia in 1909 and be black to direct or write the show, I knew there was an aspect of that which I didn't know, and I felt like I needed to have that experience and expertise in the mix.

Because my orientation is music, I started focusing on who could write the music. I met with a dozen or more people. Most everyone was intrigued and interested in *The Color Purple* and wanted to write songs on spec, which means to write a song unpaid and submit it, almost like an audition tape. I had prominent Tony Award–winning composers who did that. I had other renowned recording artists from the jazz world and the R&B world to the pop world who did that. And in the two-year period, I just didn't hear a sound that felt right. I felt like *The Color Purple* had to have its own unique sound.

I would send Alice these songs and say, "This doesn't feel right to me. What do you think?" And she would usually say, "I agree. It doesn't feel right to me, either."

ALLEE WILLIS (Songwriter): Scott and I were good friends and had done things together workwise, but never music. I had designed invitations when he was at Radio City and all kinds of other things. When he got the rights to do *The Color Purple* he called me up, and I thought, Oh, God, he's going to ask me to write the music, which would have been a dream. At that point I hadn't written music in seven years. After writing songs like "September" and "Boogie Wonderland" for Earth, Wind, and Fire, I was building alternative cyberspaces and before that I was into art. Scott knew me more in that period than he did in my very heavy music period, and the hits I had while I was friends with him were what I call my "white phase," which were for the Pet Shop Boys and the theme from *Friends*.

Scott told me he had the rights and asked me about other songwriters. I was crushed. This would have been the most perfect way back in, because I didn't know how to start writing music again. I advised him for almost a year and a half, going through names of other writers who would be appropriate. One day he called up and said, "I'm going to bounce the names of fifty songwriters off of you, and just say yes, no, as to who you think should compete," because now he was going to have people write a song on spec. When he got to the name of Brenda Russell, I thought, If I don't say something now, I'm never going to be able to.

SCOTT SANDERS: I happened to be in L.A. at the time. I called up Allee and I said, "Do you know Brenda?" And she said, "Brenda's going to be at my house in about an hour. We're writing together."

ALLEE WILLIS: She was, in fact, on her way to my house because I had co-created two animated series, one called *Fat Girl* and another one called *Driving While Black*. I was scoring both of those with Brenda [who had written "Piano in the Dark" and "Get Here," among other hits] and another writer named Stephen Bray [who wrote many songs for Madonna, including "Express Yourself" and "Into the Groove"]. So I said to Scott, "What if we compete together along with Stephen Bray?" And he said, "Okay, but no special favors." No special favors? It had been a year and a half we'd been talking about other songwriters, and he'd never mentioned me, so I certainly didn't expect a special favor at this point.

SCOTT SANDERS: I said, "I'm coming over." And I went to Allee's house, and there were Allee and Brenda and Stephen.

BRENDA RUSSELL (Songwriter): *Driving While Black* was hilarious, and we had so much fun creating the music for it. Immediately there was magic in the creative process between the three of us. One day I said, "We need something bigger." There is this wonderful principle that many of us believe in: You have to put something out there for the universe to answer you back. So when we said that, bam, here comes Scott calling Allee.

STEPHEN BRAY (Songwriter): My reaction to Scott's call was surprise because I hadn't ever done anything like that before. Certainly the word "intrigued" would probably be foremost—intrigued and also honored, of course. You don't want to be the person responsible for besmirching something so revered. I'd read the book when it came out and I'd seen the film and it was like some kind of Arthurian challenge being set before me.

SCOTT SANDERS: I brought the novel into the house, and I said, "Nine out of ten Broadway musicals fail financially. It's a tough nut to crack for someone who's done it before; it's going to be an even tougher nut to crack for someone who hasn't. But if you want to give it a shot, here's the novel. Pick any two scenes in the story to musicalize and send me the songs."

ALLEE WILLIS: Writing spec songs is not the favorite activity of songwriters and the other composers were all pretty famous, so we figured no one could really take the time, and they would probably all choose the song that Shug sang in the nightclub because that could just be a general blues song. There was no one on the list who wasn't capable of writing a great blues song or a great gospel song. We were certainly the underdogs. We really thought we needed to show that we understood characters and story arc. So we chose the area in the book where Shug Avery was going to come to town, because we thought she's so controversial that everyone in town must have an opinion of her.

BRENDA RUSSELL: It was like, "We have to have this gig." So we chose the hardest scene to write. There were multiple characters coming and going, and multiple mood changes within the scene, which we interpreted as musical changes. We wanted to demonstrate our ability to orchestrate, to really show what we had going on between the three of us.

SCOTT SANDERS: They actually wrote two songs. One was "Shug Avery Comin' to Town." The other was a song, "She Be Mine," which didn't end up in the show but was when Celie sees her daughter, Olivia, in the arms of the missionary. It's this beautiful, beautiful song, but we ended up not including that scene in the musical.

These two songs were so different and the choices of instrumentation were remarkable. I remember putting the CD on in my car and I had to pull over. I was so excited. I wanted to call them immediately on my cell phone and say, "Yay! This is it." Then I thought, No, no, no. Scott, this is a really important decision you're going to be making about who's going to write the music to *The Color Purple.* You better sleep on this.

I had friends staying at my house that weekend, and I just kept playing it on the stereo. Some of these friends had been living with the previous submissions and people were dancing around the house, saying, "Oh my God! This is so great!"

I sent it to Alice and Alice called back and said, "I think this is it." I said, "I do too."

Gary Griffin

I called them and said, "If you can do twenty more of these, you've got the job."

THE DEVELOPMENT

Finding the Right Director

GARY GRIFFIN (Director): Scott and I had been talking about working on something together. Then he called and told me one of the projects he was working on was *The Color Purple.* I immediately thought for many reasons it was a good idea. It's a strong, powerful, emotionally gripping story, a big story, a story of the triumph of the human spirit. All things that make a good musical. It also offers an interesting challenge in making Celie, a character who could perceptively be passive, come to the forefront and be at the center of a big musical. I think to really do a project, you want to find the thing that poses the greatest challenge, because that's what's going to make the job interesting.

There are things musical theater can and can't do. More than anything, musical theater can risk a heightened emotional moment, and moments in a story that have heightened emotional payoffs. In a movie or a play, a scene played extremely well can begin to stir your spirit. But in musical theater, because it's the confluence of music and words and character, the spiritual part of theater comes alive. So in adapting the story, we looked at the moments that lent themselves best to musical theater. To me, it felt like a big act of sculpture. I never thought we were making *The Color Purple* into a musical. I felt like we were taking away everything from *The Color Purple* that wasn't a musical, and chipping away at events that, in the world of musical theater, probably wouldn't land.

Marsha Norman

MARSHA NORMAN JOINS THE TEAM

MARSHA NORMAN (Book Writer): I've been trying to say yes to *The Color Purple* since 1983. When Spielberg was getting ready to do the movie, he called me—well, I need to go back further than that. When Alice and I won the Pulitzers on the same day, our names were together on the bottom right-hand corner of the *New York Times*. "Norman and Walker win Pulitzers for drama and fiction." I loved her book, and I loved what I knew about her. And I just felt like we were somehow allied.

So when Spielberg called and said, "Would you come out and talk to me about writing the movie of *The Color Purple*?" I said, "Yeah, yeah, yeah, yes, yes, yes."

I arrived out there and got into the long car he sent for me. I had done a lot of work to get ready, and I had ideas about what needed to be done to make it a movie. We had about forty-five minutes of this conversation, and it was clear almost immediately that he did not want me.

He said to me that my play *'Night, Mother* had a lot of pretty writing in it, but how could she do that to her mother? So he really just didn't want me; that was clear. I was disappointed, but when we left his office, Quincy Jones, who had been in the room with us as Alice's representative, invited me to lunch. Now, this never happens. You don't get rejected from a job and then Quincy Jones asks you to lunch. And we went to a French restaurant he knew and had this wonderful lunch talking about Petula Clark and Michael Jackson. I got to say what his work had done for me, and I got to ask all these crazy fan questions. It was wonderful. And then I got back in the car and went back to the airport and back home, and that was the end.

Five or six years ago, when I heard they were working on the musical, I put my hand in the air again and I said, "Oh, me, me, pick me." They got back in touch with my agent and me and said, "No, no, we can't have you; we need a black writer." And I said, "Well, of course you do." And I wished them luck and that was it.

And then I got this strange phone call in February of 2005, right before I was getting ready to leave for Paris: Could I come in to this workshop on Monday? They had a whole cast and a whole score and they're starting on Monday, but they had no book, would I come? And I said, "Yes, yes, yes."

GARY GRIFFIN: Our music team is extraordinarily gifted, and they wrote amazing songs. Our challenge and our struggle was that distinction between this is a great song but not the song for this moment. Or our show's too long. Or we have too many songs like this in a row. That's what's so heartbreaking and difficult: You're taking away something that is amazingly powerful and beautiful, but because of where it's living in the show, it's not paying off, or it's something we're giving focus to that the audience really isn't interested in.

MARSHA NORMAN: One of the things a musical book writer has to do is to figure out who is the chorus, what is the chorus, and how do we get the chorus on stage? The big thing about the South, which I knew from growing up there, is everybody knows who you are and what you're doing and what you're up against and how you're faring. And because it's a world that's lived outside and in a sense of familiarity, you're constantly being watched.

In this particular case, I felt that they're watching Celie because she's doing something really different than girls have normally done. She's not one of these crazy people like Sofia. That's not who Celie is. Celie is a normal girl who is writing her own *Feminine Mystique*. Celie is stepping into a freedom that girls have not had in her part of the world. And she's going to end up a prosperous businesswoman, and she's going to end up the center of a great group of people. An image I had that Gary really picked up on, and we really worked hard on together, was this image of a bird in a tree. In the beginning, what we see is the girls in the tree, and they're completely by themselves. And we know from various things that happen during the story that Celie does identify with birds—she sings in that first song that she wants to raise birds. By the end, what you see is that Celie basically has become the tree. And everybody has come back to roost in the branches of Celie. The whole family has, as if they've all taken refuge and shelter in her. She has become the family tree.

STEPHEN BRAY: The songwriting we were used to allows you so much more freedom because you really don't have to make a lot of sense. You can write a lyric that is really simple and is just pleasing to hear. You know, "Sugar / Oh Honey, honey / You are my candy girl / And you got me wantin' you." For me, that's a very pleasurable piece of music.

Duke Ellington's wonderful quote is, "If it sounds good, it is good." It's true when you're talking about music for music's sake. But when you add the drama to it, the theater to it, you need to be bringing a whole other art form and a whole other blending of idioms and it can't just sound good.

Musical theater is another ballgame. When we started out, the people who really knew would say to us, "This is great-sounding music but you're going to have to change it." And we cockily said, "Oh no, people love the songs," because we had a lot of demos right off the bat that people were telling us were really beautiful. But when you had to put it on the beat, as we like to say in the theater, the proof would be in the pudding, and it wasn't a lot of times. So we had to learn.

MARSHA NORMAN: What I did a lot with Brenda, Allee, and Stephen was to say what the dramatic content of the lyrics had to be, and where it had to end up. It's like hooking up train cars. Pop writers are used to writing songs that finish, and then there's nothing.

BRENDA RUSSELL: The leap was telling the specific story and having it move forward. That was a huge challenge. If Celie's standing in the middle of the stage, you don't want her to sing, "And I'm standing here wondering," because you're seeing it. You don't want her singing, "You walked out on me," when she just walked out. You have to make the action move forward, and you have to make it sound like that character.

ALLEE WILLIS: A lot of times if you lyrically change one thing in the story, it's a domino effect. Melodies that worked become too melancholy, or too insistent. The biggest lesson we had to learn was to not say it's a good song. Don't say it's such a great song. It's whether the song is telling the story effectively.

BRENDA RUSSELL: I think the hardest challenge was to rewrite something that you loved. I'm used to people saying yea or nay, but not "Rewrite." It was hard to adapt to that when you loved a song, you knew it was great, or you believed in it. You had to just let that go, and that was, to me, very difficult. We got really good at

"By the end what you see is that Celie basically has become the tree. And everyone has come back to roost in the branches of Celie."

— MARSHA NORMAN

it near the end. It used to be this agonizing, artistic suffering, and then it got to be, "Okay, what else? Next?"

MARSHA NORMAN: When I came in, there were a lot of songs written. They had written "What About Love?" They had written "Shug Avery Comin' to Town." They'd written "Hell No." But a lot were written as stand-alones. My task was to figure out how to pull them into the story so that they didn't seem like, "And here comes the song!" In other words, "Shug Avery Comin' to Town," was originally just, "Shug Avery's coming to town, she's coming to town, she's coming to town."

What I was able to do there was to say, "No, no, Shug Avery coming to town means two really different things depending on whether you're men or women." And since we've got such a big gender difference going on, this is the perfect song to make it clear that the women view this as a real threat, and the men view this as a great thing. And to use that as the central, macro drama, which is exemplified by Celie and Mister in the micro realm, about what is this woman going to mean in our lives? So you have the women singing, "Lock up all your men." But it's what Celie is struggling with, "This man who's been so horrible to me, am I gonna lose him now? Is that what's gonna happen?" So part of what I did with those songs that already existed was to try to figure out how they became part of the show, instead of isolated performance moments.

"Shug Avery coming to town means two really different things depending on whether you're men or women... So you have the women singing, 'Lock ups all your men!'"

—MARSHA NORMAN

ATLANTA

SCOTT SANDERS: In creating this musical, we had to decide early on, Is this going to be a book musical? Or is it going to be sung through like *Les Misérables*, which doesn't go back and forth between scenes and songs? And so we just decided to write it and let it evolve organically and figure out what it was going to be later. Then when we were writing we thought, Okay, at some point, we're going to have to put this in front of an audience and see how it's working and whether they're responding to the material.

There are wonderful regional not-for-profit theaters around the United States that excel at developing material and at presenting new work prior to coming to Broadway. Susan Booth of the Alliance Theatre actively pursued us, which I really admired, because she took as great a leap of faith as anyone else on us. She had heard some songs and read an early draft of the script but she had no idea where this thing would go, either. And it felt like going back to Georgia, to the roots of the story, was a good idea. I met with her in Atlanta, and left the theater and called Alice. I said, "I think this is where we're going."

CAMILLE LOVE (Director, Atlanta Bureau of Cultural Affairs): Those of us who are from the South really love the South, and we are not that distant from that rural scene: You can probably find some pocket communities where the entire family lives on the same street, they all belong to the same church, the church is the center, and their lives are very much involved in that little insular community. The themes in *The Color Purple* are recurring themes—they're not just set in the period of time or place—but for us they really are Southern, and they are alive and well, and we can connect with them even today.

SUSAN BOOTH (Artistic Director, Alliance Theatre): Atlanta is the African-American mecca. It's a city that is both uniquely defined by regional specificity and an enormous transplanted population. So finding a work that can sit in our space and speak to the diversity, the multiplicity of this city in a common language is a rare and wonderful thing. Particularly during the preview period, our audience tells us what they appreciate, what they are challenged by, what's clear, and what's not clear, purely by dint of their collective response. And unexpected moments are core to the process.

GARY GRIFFIN: We made tons of discoveries in Atlanta, mostly having to do with the opening. In Atlanta, the opening started at a funeral. I don't want to say it was depressing, but I don't think the audience connected to the universe of the play as well as the opening now, which is in the spirit of the church. A major part of the survival of the community is how they live in the world of the church.

RUDOLPH P. BYRD (Professor of American Studies, Emory University): I wanted to be supportive of this production. My specialization is twentieth-century African-American literature, so I routinely teach Alice's work. This was a hugely important cultural event for the region, for the nation, and also for the Alliance Theatre, because this production conjures up the debates that took place during the 1980s following not only the publication of the novel, but also the film adaptation by Steven Spielberg.

No writer in the twentieth century was attacked in the sustained and virulent way that Alice was around this novel. No writer. None. The critique was that Alice Walker and her novel were committed only to an unfair representation of the lives of black men. Feminists at that time were perceived—and still are—as hostile to the black liberation struggle.

Spielberg's film was gasoline that spread that fire. In the critics' view, the film portrayed Mister and other African-American men in the novel as misogynistic, as haters and beaters of women. I wondered if the play would generate a similar response, and I was delighted that it did not. The play was well received here in Atlanta. It was beautifully adapted at the Alliance Theatre, and I went to see it six times.

STEPHEN BRAY: One of the jobs of an opening is supposedly to give a quick jolt of what you can expect for the evening. Is it going to be serious? Is it going to be silly? Is the music going to be orchestral? Is the music going to be bluesy? The revised opener lets you realize that the show's going to be deep but it's going to be fun, too.

ALICE WALKER: Scott lost weight sitting next to me in Atlanta. Poor dear, he wanted us to sit together. You know that thing about George Washington saying, "I cannot tell a lie?" Well I really can't. I knew that I would have to tell the truth, and I was so sorry that he was sitting there. And the first feeling of anything is so difficult, because it's really hard to see the completed thing separate from all that had gone before. This happened with the film, too. So that was very hard. I liked it, but I wasn't wholehearted.

SCOTT SANDERS: I'm sitting with her opening night. And she's very quiet through the entire show. Doesn't speak much at intermission. Certainly doesn't talk about her feelings about the show, and at the end of the show, doesn't say anything, gets up, and leaves.

I thought, She needs to think about it. But the next day, I don't hear from her at all. And she's now going to the show the second night. And I'm dying. The whole day, I'm thinking, She hates it. What is going on? What are we going to do? Everybody is calling me. Allee Willis is calling and Gary Griffin's calling, everybody's calling, What did Alice think? What did Alice say? I don't know, she hasn't told me. What do you mean she hasn't told you? She didn't say anything? And then we all started getting paranoid thinking that Alice didn't like it.

Plus, I had said to her, "If you don't like it, we won't do it." So I'm thinking, Oh my God.

When she came the second night, I just steered clear of her. I threw a little reception afterward, she came to that, and one of her friends came over and said, "Alice wants to see you."

ALICE WALKER: It took the second evening of seeing the show—just as it had taken a second viewing of the film—to really see it. This has nothing to do with anything missing in the production. It had only to do with my own need to let all previous things fall away so that I could see what they were actually offering.

The second night I thought it was fabulous. I loved it. In fact, I loved it so much I was afraid they would ruin it when they came to Broadway. I thought, Oh dear, this was so beautiful.

SCOTT SANDERS: The Atlanta run was five weeks, and I brought the creative team back in for the last week of shows. The day after the last show, we sat and did six hours of notes. We went scene by scene and talked about what we wanted to change for Broadway. I called Alice right after we closed in Atlanta, and I said, "We're going to go back and take nine months and rewrite, and then we're going to do a workshop of the rewritten material." I remember she said, "Don't screw it up."

CONVINCING OTHER PRODUCERS TO SIGN ON

ROY FURMAN (Producer): When I told Scott I'd be interested, I meant it. But I had no idea to what degree. I went down to see it in Atlanta and I was appalled.

The show opened with a funeral, the chorus was in black, they walked on stage, and from that moment on it just went down, until Sofia came in. Then came the second act, and I found myself, by the end of the show, crying, and everyone else in the audience crying. This is a show I knew, a book I'd read, a movie I'd seen, and it still caught me so unaware. Afterward I met with Gary and Scott and told them how much I disliked the first act, and Scott told me later that he was positive that I was about to do the old fade. I explained why I didn't like it and what was wrong, and then I said, "But I have to tell you something. If the show has such power that it could get me to cry despite not liking one of its two acts, then I recognize what it would mean when you get the act right."

And therefore, I said, "I'm in." We came back to New York. Scott said, "Look, I can't raise money. I don't know this world, and you do. Why don't we be fifty-fifty partners, and you help raise the money and work with me on the show?" I agreed to do it on the spot. The big money people saw the workshops, loved it, and then gave a hundred reasons why they couldn't do it, none of which were the truth. They'd walk out and say, "Well, I don't know," "I'm not sure," I'm this, I'm that. But the fact is, it was not easy, and we ended up funding this outside the mainstream of Broadway.

QUINCY JONES (Producer): Roy Furman kept asking me to do it, and I told him I had too much stuff going on. And Scott came out to L.A. and talked to me about it. I said, "What do we have to do?" They said, "First, we have to get a theater." There's only two places to go [for theater space on Broadway], and that's the Nederlanders and the Schuberts. So I called Jimmy Nederlander and he said, "We don't have the theaters." I've known him a long time. And I'd just seen Gerry Schoenfeld, from the Schubert theaters, in Positano where I had just been on a trip to the Amalfi Coast. I called him, and he says, "I can't do it because we're doing *Mambo Kings*." Then, unfortunately, *Mambo Kings* closed in San Francisco after five days. He called back and said, "You got it. But it's going to cost you. You have to do a month in one of my theaters with your band and some singers." I said, "We'll talk about that later."

ROY FURMAN: This is a prejudiced country, and we can deny it, but then we're being liars, frankly. Even people who are liberal and fair-minded are, in ways, prejudiced. One reason I loved *The Color Purple* was because it's not black and white. This is the world that all people live in. All these difficulties—of battered wives or finding one's self—you don't have to be black, you can be anybody.

When I first presented this idea to potential investors, even my Broadway newcomers said they didn't think this was a subject for a musical because it involved lesbianism and all kinds of neglect, abuse, and child separation. I said, "If you don't want to invest in this, I have another one. It's a musical; you're going to love it. It's got a lot of comedy, and it's about Jews in Russia who are being persecuted. They're attacked by the czar, and they're beaten and abused and they have terrible relationships. Very exciting first act ends with their entire village ransacked in a pogrom. The second act is even better. They all get kicked out of the town." I said, "If you think that way, no musical could work. But the fact is, creative genius can do anything." I used that as a way to get people to invest. They got it right away. In the right hands, almost anything can work. The irony is that people now come back and say, "This is the black *Fiddler on the Roof*." Big stories are small stories told large, and that's what this is.

QUINCY JONES: There has never been a better cast on the stage in the history of Broadway, I don't think. You cry twelve times. It moved me. It knocked my socks off. It really got to us all. The naysayers or whatever, they were wrong. And they said that black people wouldn't come to see it. Wrong.

Sitzprobe is a German term that means to sit and work. That's what happened here, and after separate rehearsals for weeks on end, the cast and the eighteen-piece orchestra finally came together one afternoon to sing through the entire show for the first time.

"The thrill of the sitzprobe is to finally hear the music fleshed out for a full orchestra," says Kevin Stites, the show's music supervisor. "So things that were just clunky notes or percussive chords on the rehearsal piano are now strings passages or brass instruments. It's like when Dorothy wakes up and exits the house into Munchkinland. All of a sudden, it's color. It's Technicolor."

This page, top image, from left: Linda Twine, Kenita R. Miller, Allee Willis, LaChanze, and Brenda Russell; middle image: Brenda Russell; bottom image: Charles LaPointe and Felicia P. Fields. Opposite page, top image, from left: Kenita R. Miller, Allee Willis, LaChanze, and Brenda Russell; middle image: Kenita R. Miller; bottom image: Gary Griffin.

THE WRITING

MARSHA NORMAN: In Alice's version, Celie watches the whole time. She's the recording secretary. She writes it all down. Things happen to her, but other characters are way flashier and way funnier and way more the attention-getters. One thing we had to do was to keep Celie at the front, see the whole thing through Celie's eyes so that she can sing that big song at the end, "I'm Beautiful and I'm Here." I had to rejigger, as my granddaddy used to say, this story. When Sofia sings about violence, she sings it to Celie. Instead of Sofia proclaiming about how violence is bad, she sings it to Celie because she's noticed how Mister treats her and she wants Celie to be free. Everything points to Celie. That's the main thing that we had to do for her.

In the beginning, Celie sings to her child, "Somebody's gonna love you." In the scene after that, she says, "I can't have no more children; I guess God just wants me to take care of things." She's not thinking about herself. She's looking out for other people in the world; her baby, her sister, her aunt, Mister's kids, all this. But by the end of the story, she's able to take care of herself. To love herself. She's able to say, "I'm beautiful and I'm here." She's able to say, "I've got everything in me that I need to live a bountiful life." She says to Shug, "I don't need you to love me; I don't need you to love. I got my sister, I got my children, I got my hands, I got my house." She's come around to this understanding of the beauty in her. She no longer has to be told that she's beautiful or worth fighting for. She knows it. She has fallen in love with herself. She has come into this great, deep, profound love for the gift of her own life.

This is an awakening. Celie wakes up to what we have all known since moment one of the show. We have all loved her since the beginning. And now she comes to love her. In the end it's this sort of a romance. It's, "Oh, wait, finally these people find each other: It's Celie and herself."

In a way, part of it is what you get and what you get free of. Celie gets out of Mister's house and gets into Shug's life. Into Shug's house. Then Celie gets her house, she gets a business, she makes a go of this business, and then she gets free of Shug. Finally, Celie is left with herself and comes to this blinding understanding that that's exactly where she would most want to be. And once she arrives at this moment when she feels she's completely able to go on by herself in happiness and peace, then she gets the great gift of getting her sister back.

One of the hardest things that we had to struggle with was how to incorporate Celie into the Africa story. So that when you have Celie and Nettie standing there with those women talking to them, the full impact of the scene is not just that they emerge from Africa, but it's the fact that Celie is there, too. Nettie has no way of knowing about these gossips. Celie sees one group of women who are truly African and who are truly outraged about teaching girls to read. Celie also sees this echo of the women whom she has known her whole life. And suddenly, the audience says, Oh, these women are everywhere. So it's like three separate perceptions of that role of the Church Ladies, as they're called.

And the great breakthrough in Africa was equating Africa with Sofia. When you say, Okay, Africa is Sofia, then you really can get that here's this great big powerful force that's also vulnerable to great harm.

ALICE WALKER: What I like most about Marsha's work is that she was very respectful of what was already there and had a real sense of the modernity. She brought that out in a good way, because many people see it as a period piece that's somewhat static; they don't see that the people are developing both in terms of a contemporary spirituality and into people who could be very happy contemporarily. The way Harpo and Sofia live isn't stuck in time. It's a sustainable, egalitarian model of a marriage and a family. And one of the very sweet things they did was to have Harpo bonding with this last child of Sofia's, Henrietta, and we know she's not his child. So that again brings us to this sense of the contemporary of how people live now and how families are made. As opposed to how they used to be: If you had an "illegitimate child" you'd always beat up on it or whatever. No. Harpo has decided and his heart has decided he loves his mate and he loves this child and he's going to help them and he's going to be with them.

And that's the model that we can sustain and we can actually use to survive this period we're in, which is one of the worst periods that the world has ever known. And that is why we also need art like this. We need art that affirms that we can transform enough to survive and to thrive.

SCOTT SANDERS: We are dealing with much more complicated storytelling in *The Color Purple* than a lot of musicals. Just like *Les Misérables*, which packs in a whole bunch of material, I mean, I needed to see it three times just to pick up all the pieces.

I'm sure some critics would have preferred that we narrow the focus of our storytelling. I think we did the best job we possibly could have, condensing all that material and telling that story in two hours and forty minutes. But it definitely does require you to pay attention and to think. It's not boy meets girl, boy loses girl, boy gets girl. That's not what *The Color Purple* is.

PUTTING TOGETHER A COHESIVE SHOW

SCOTT SANDERS: We had a self-imposed mandate that we were going to stay as true to the book and the story as humanly possible. If we couldn't tell *The Color Purple*, if it didn't work as a musical, we just wouldn't do it. But we weren't going to tell a different story. It was about respecting the place that the book had in the world. In order for me to have the right to do this, I owed everyone who loved *The Color Purple* to do it as true to the original story as we possibly could. Some of the criticism we've gotten was that we have too much material in the show, it's too much for people to digest, and it moves too quickly. We thought a lot about that. Do we need Squeak in the show at all? Should this be only Nettie and Celie's story and everybody else becomes secondary? Do we need to give Mister a redemption song? But Alice gave us so many rich stories; every single principal character has an amazing forty-year character arc and growth arc. A lot of shows have a protagonist doing all the growth and the change, and everybody else is window dressing. Alice didn't give us a story like that.

"A lot of shows have a protagonist doing all the growth and change, and everbody else is window dressing. Alice didn't give us a story like that."

— SCOTT SANDERS

ALLEE WILLIS: One question was always, How important are all of these B stories, like Sofia and Harpo? But you know what? This is not the Anne Frank story, you know what I mean? This is about a community and this woman who really becomes the center of this whole community—how important human connection is. All of these people having all of these stories, that's how Celie learns. She watched Sofia and she watched Shug and she watched Nettie and took teeny pieces of all of them, and then, when she finally found herself, used that to color everything.

SCOTT SANDERS: When you make creative choices, you're kind of damned if you do and damned if you don't. Alice Walker wanted to see the relationship between Celie and Shug Avery more fully developed in the musical. We wanted to tell that story. We also wanted to show Harpo's growth. We wanted to show more than just the one-dimensional guy who's willing to marry the strong woman. That's the easy part of him. Clearly the song late in the second act, "Any Little Thing," could have been cut and no one would have felt from a storytelling point of view that we owed the audience anything.

The thing that's so great about this story in 2006 is that it shows the world that the family never was *Leave It to Beaver*. It never was *Father Knows Best*. It's always been more complicated than that. These characters move around in love. They move around in anger. They move around in growth. That's reality and that's life, and even though this story was told within the period of 1909 to 1949, it's still, in so many ways, timeless, because life doesn't fit into neat little boxes. It just doesn't.

MARSHA NORMAN: We wanted to return to the book in its treatment of the men: We wanted to give Mister his full journey, which is all the way through to his redemption, to where he understands. In the book, there's actually a lot more about what Mister does for Henrietta. Alice feels strongly that Henrietta is his path to redemption. And that line about "It's time I did something nice for some little girl"? That's my line, not Alice's, but it's a summary of what Alice was saying about what Mister realizes is his way back. And so he's able to ask Celie to marry him at the end and also to do the work to bring her sister back. He really makes his amends. And she is able to accept them.

We had cut down that final picnic scene between Mister and Celie, and we had cut out the line, "Us lived through it." And the whole thing didn't work. It just didn't work. The business about the shell and the bird, we'd taken all that out, and with it had gone the line, "Us lived through it." It turned out that Celie needed a moment in the show when she not necessarily forgave Mister, but indicated that it was all right for them to begin the next stage of their relationship.

She says she doesn't want to marry him, but she does say, "Us lived through it." I think this is the incredible moment of grace on her part, an incredible sense of, Well, truly what matters is that we're both still standing up. And we did get through that. And you were horrible. But you know that now.

"She says she doesn't want to marry him, but she does say, 'Us lived through it.'"

— MARSHA NORMAN

D.P. Thomson
1118 WALNUT ST.

Chapter Two

The Songs

WRITING THE SONGS

ALICE WALKER: When Allee would send me stuff, I would get it, and when friends would come over, often we would end up playing the music and dancing. We just had a wonderful time and loved the music long before the play opened.

I went [to L.A.] and basically had council with Stephen and Allee and Brenda. Long discussions about what worked and what didn't. But more than that, discussions about the life vision in the work. It was important for me that they didn't end up with something that just reinforced people's original religious thinking, because that would have been, for me, failure.

People have to be moved from whatever they think of as theirs, which they only inherited. I mean, it's subtle, but it's really in the novel: You don't have to be, but you're challenged to consider moving from what has been so comfortable—you know, the old-time religion—into a different way of looking at the world, which hopefully will mean a dedication to saving it. Because the religion that we inherited talks about dominion of the earth. Which we have had dominion of to its peril. It's so dominated that we have very little of it left. And that has to change if we're going to survive. We won't survive on this old-time religion where man gets to just do whatever he wants. That is over. And so we had talks like that.

I remember one meeting we had just before the show opened in New York. They had a song in which Celie was singing about "being in your hands" and reaching up toward the sky. That was not right for this piece. Because it reinforces the stereotype of a God that actually has hands. Some big man with his hands holding you. Well no, that is not what we have here. And I have to say that Stephen, Allee, and Brenda were right there with me in the most phenomenal way.

STEPHEN BRAY (Songwriter): Allee told us that Alice basically had to put herself in a state and receive the story. Thank God Brenda comes from that kind of place and she led the charge with making sure that we just received the music. Allee and I were both open to taking that on as a real process.

BRENDA RUSSELL (Songwriter): Whenever I sat at the piano, I would call it, for the lack of a better term, sort of like channeling. I would open myself up to say, Okay, what do you want to say? I always tried to get out of the way, because that is how I do my best writing anyway. Get out of the way and let it come through you. But you have to know that exists in order to utilize it. Once you understand that it's not all about you, it's you opening to that elusive thing called creation, then you can count on it. And that's what I did, I counted on it. And it always came through. I'm not saying that it was always great. I'm just saying that it always came through for me.

STEPHEN BRAY: Brenda would begin to hear what the musical atmosphere was very quickly. That's the car Brenda drives, and Allee typically will be riding along. Now, at different points, to wear out the analogy, any of us could be in the passenger seat saying, I think you should turn left here, keep going straight. Because that is really what happens with the way we work: Allee might be driving the melody of the car but then we'll say, Oh, that's too weird. Or that's not emotionally right. It shifts around a lot, and that's the beauty of having three people in a room.

BRENDA RUSSELL: I liked the trio because if two people disagree about something, you can get into a stalemate; with three people it's a democracy. And it's buoyant: Two people can get bogged down sometimes, with three people there's always someone saying, Oh, what about this? It was both fun and we had our moments of…"intensity." That is always going to happen. There's always going to be a little tension, but that's part of the creative process. Plus, I don't think any of us have ever worked so hard and so long on one project. I'm amazed at how well we did, actually, considering how intense it all was. And we all still love each other.

UNITED STATES POSTAGE
3 CENTS 3
W. C. Williams

ALLEE WILLIS (Songwriter): "Mysterious Ways" came after Atlanta. Brenda, Stephen, Marsha, Gary, and I were pretty certain in Atlanta that we didn't have the right opening, or the right song, or anything. So we already knew before that run even ended, that everything up until "Hell No!" was going to change. "Mysterious Ways" came out of a discussion that we had, to set up what Celie was up against in her life—not just this chain of abusive men, but this whole societal way of thinking that the afterlife was the only place you were supposed to find peace. Therefore, whatever abuse you had to endure in life was okay, and it was justified, because your payoff wasn't coming on this plane. So many people are familiar with that expression, "God works in mysterious ways." We thought that was a great way of setting it up so that you saw this very commonplace, rural mindset.

GARY GRIFFIN (Director): The song and the handclaps that the little girls start off with was important because I wanted the audience to remember this story started with little girls. These girls take a journey, but they were little girls in a tree at one point. I wanted that burned into your soul as you watched the show. That was the first thing you heard. It was the little girls and the sound of the church, and that's where it started.

BRENDA RUSSELL: On "Huckleberry Pie," Allee and I were like two little schoolgirls singing, "Hey, sista, watcha gon do...." We always knew the handclaps had to be a part of that. That was just understood. It didn't originally combine with "Mysterious Ways," which we wrote a few years into the process. They said, "We need something more interesting in this opening," and we felt that, too. We often referred to old gospel records. We'd listen and get the feel, and just drown ourselves in that style. So Stephen and I found this gospel rhythm, and we started foot-stomping, and singing our hearts out to this music. That was one of the most fun songs to write.

STEPHEN BRAY: This song teaches you right off the bat what Celie's about, that her nature is compassionate and loving in the extreme.

BRENDA RUSSELL: I was just kind of humming at the piano, and Allee said, "That's it! That's good!" and I said, "No, I have to work on it, I have to fiddle with it and mess with it." Working with these people taught me, No, you don't. Sometimes the first idea is really good. Go with it.

ALLEE WILLIS: In Atlanta, we saw Celie pregnant and then the next minute she wasn't. We never saw this personal relationship that she had with the baby. We felt that to understand the stakes of getting her babies back, you had to see her connection with one of them. So we decided to write just a little lullaby, and it should be a cappella, because that was about as personal as it could get.

ALLEE WILLIS: From a fictional place, the main story is these two sisters get separated, then they get back together. Before Atlanta, Nettie and Celie never had a song together. So we felt like we had to show what they meant to each other, and that their prayer was that God would somehow keep them together.

STEPHEN BRAY: The sisters sing, and then Mister comes in singing about wanting to marry Nettie. I love that it's like, Oh, where do I pay my attention? The back and forth juxtaposing of the girls' innocence and his malevolent sneer.

BRENDA RUSSELL: They were two different songs that were put together, and Allee was really good at that. She would always hear it. "It will work," she'd say.

ALLEE WILLIS: Counterpoints are the stuff real musical theater is made of. A lot of times, in great musicals like *Fiddler on the Roof*, they'll have four and five people singing at the same time. There are melodies connected to specific characters that you pre–establish, then it's up to the audience who to listen to. That's difficult because on the one hand you need everything to come across, and on the other hand, if you have four and five, or even two actors singing at the same time, a lot of people aren't going to grasp everything that everyone is saying. So somehow in the musical tone of what you're doing, you've got to get across the emotion of what someone's trying to say.

BRENDA RUSSELL: We were trying to tell some part of the story, and we didn't know which character was going to relate this information. I just said, "Why don't we have three women do it?" It just came out, and that was the birth of the Church Ladies. Allee came up with the major hook of the Church Ladies: "I heard about po' chile Celie." She started singing that, and we were like, "Yeah. We'll do that." Everybody loved it so much, they'd say, "Let's have them do another thing," and it became the Greek chorus.

ALLEE WILLIS: The Church Ladies' job was that they were the obvious humor in the show, so how do you make it funny, ballsy, but get this information across? They became a way to eliminate a lot of dialogue and bring you up to speed on everyone's emotional state. So that becomes a big task. In most of their sections each one only has one line. They repeat it over and over, so you always have to say a lot with very little, and you have to get across these very serious facts but make it funny.

STEPHEN BRAY: We wrote a lot of the material for a year and a half in Allee's converted bedroom studio, and it sounded good to us and so we thought it was good. We're okay with that. That's cute. We think that's amusing. But when it came to life, and the actual Church Ladies who'd been cast gave it their flavor, it just exploded. We couldn't wait to write more pieces for them. It's one thing when you're by yourself in the studio. We can make it sound okay, but the actors bring it to life. They gave it so much more than I ever imagined.

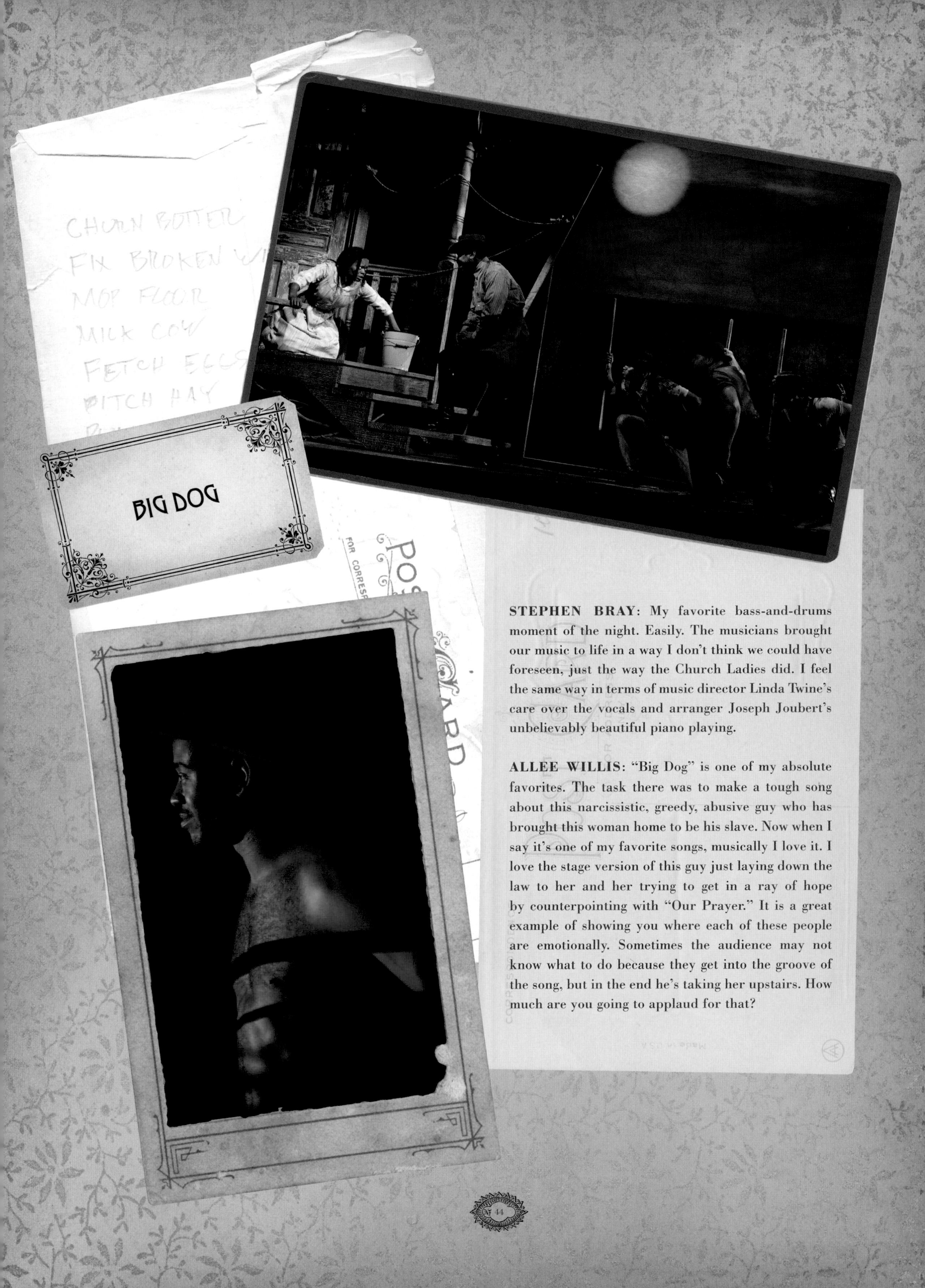

STEPHEN BRAY: My favorite bass-and-drums moment of the night. Easily. The musicians brought our music to life in a way I don't think we could have foreseen, just the way the Church Ladies did. I feel the same way in terms of music director Linda Twine's care over the vocals and arranger Joseph Joubert's unbelievably beautiful piano playing.

ALLEE WILLIS: "Big Dog" is one of my absolute favorites. The task there was to make a tough song about this narcissistic, greedy, abusive guy who has brought this woman home to be his slave. Now when I say it's one of my favorite songs, musically I love it. I love the stage version of this guy just laying down the law to her and her trying to get in a ray of hope by counterpointing with "Our Prayer." It is a great example of showing you where each of these people are emotionally. Sometimes the audience may not know what to do because they get into the groove of the song, but in the end he's taking her upstairs. How much are you going to applaud for that?

Dear God,
I never ask for anything,
but I'm asking for this.
If I'm really a lily
of the field, you will
answer my prayers—
or you're no God at all!

STEPHEN BRAY: Celie sings, "If I'm really a lily of the field, you will answer my prayer." In rehearsal it used to be impossible to watch LaChanze do that without crying. She's acting it day after day in rehearsal after rehearsal, scene after scene. She would get down on the floor and it just hurt to watch her do it. So that moment—a total Allee melody, by the way—was really powerful.

Celie's saying, Consider the lilies of the field. They don't do anything, neither do they spin, neither do they toil, and God takes care of them. It's about being part of God's creation and being nurtured as such.

I cannot tell you how strongly some people wanted to get rid of it because they felt that it was a complete non sequitur, that no one would understand it or get the feeling. But I was ready to fight hard for it.

BRENDA RUSSELL: I was on his side on that one. All three of us loved it but when we had to deal with the rest of the creative team, we would have to fight for things. There were tears shed. I remember one reading that was very difficult. People we're saying, We're cutting this, we're cutting that, we're cutting this. I had to get up and walk out so I could cry. I was just hysterical in the hallway, and then Marsha came out and said, "It's going to be okay, honey." I said, "They can't, they can't cut this." You get so wrapped up in the music that it becomes part of your blood, and it's hard to let go of certain things.

ALLEE WILLIS: If I'm in the mood, then it's just turn on the mike, I have no idea what's about to come out. A lot of stuff was written that way. Like the verses of "Hell No!" That was the first one where we had an instinct that it wasn't going to rhyme, but it still had to be a song. How do you write a verse without it rhyming and not sounding stupid? I just picked up Alice's book and flipped between three or four pages, and as this melody was coming to me, the words spoke to me, and it worked.

BRENDA RUSSELL: We wanted it to be anthemic, especially for women who are abused. We wanted that to be a song that makes everybody stand up and raise their fists in the air and go, "Oh, yeah!" Everybody can sing along if they want to, and it's something that everyone can relate to and is moved by. We had so much fun. I think half the fun was recording our demos. Alice still misses our demos. It's so cute. She's like, "I miss hearing you guys sing those songs," because we sang everything together. Stephen had to be the woman all the time; we'd make him sing high. He was also the great preacher voice.

STEPHEN BRAY: I saw it the first time it was sung in front of an audience in Atlanta. When you look up the phrase "instant gratification" in the dictionary, there should be a hologram of that first time Sofia sings, "Hell No!" and then you'd get to hear what happens in the room. Because you don't know it's coming. There is a certain sound when you have, say, a hundred women letting out the same sound, like an "Ohhhh!" or an "Unh!" or a "Mm-mm-mm." For me—I have a black mom, black parents, and being a black guy—that sound goes right into my cellular memory of hearing the family all together and something happens and everybody goes, "Oh Lord, child." That's what it was like. It was like hearing a thousand—well, it was only six hundred in Atlanta, but it seemed like six thousand—people doing that at the same time. That was beautiful.

BROWN BETTY

BRENDA RUSSELL: We wanted this to have a chain-gang feeling. At Allee's house, we had egg beaters and pots and pans—things that sounded like tools. That was the essence of that song—bomp, bomp, bah—the sounds of building the juke joint. We would be banging on all kinds of things. We'd drag out washboards, and we had everything going on.

STEPHEN BRAY: At first it was an innocent paean to the old work songs, the railroad song, just any song to keep your mind off the fact that you were standing in 110 degrees picking cotton and cutting your fingers. Then as we got deeper into the project, we realized we can't spare any moments where we're doing that pop thing, where we're doing something that sounds good and feels good. It can't just be about those two elements. We need to learn something from it. There was a lot of discussion on whether or not that song was just a work song or did it tell a story? I'll admit I was on the wrong side of that argument for a little while. But I'm happy to say I saw the light.

SHUG AVERY COMIN' TO TOWN

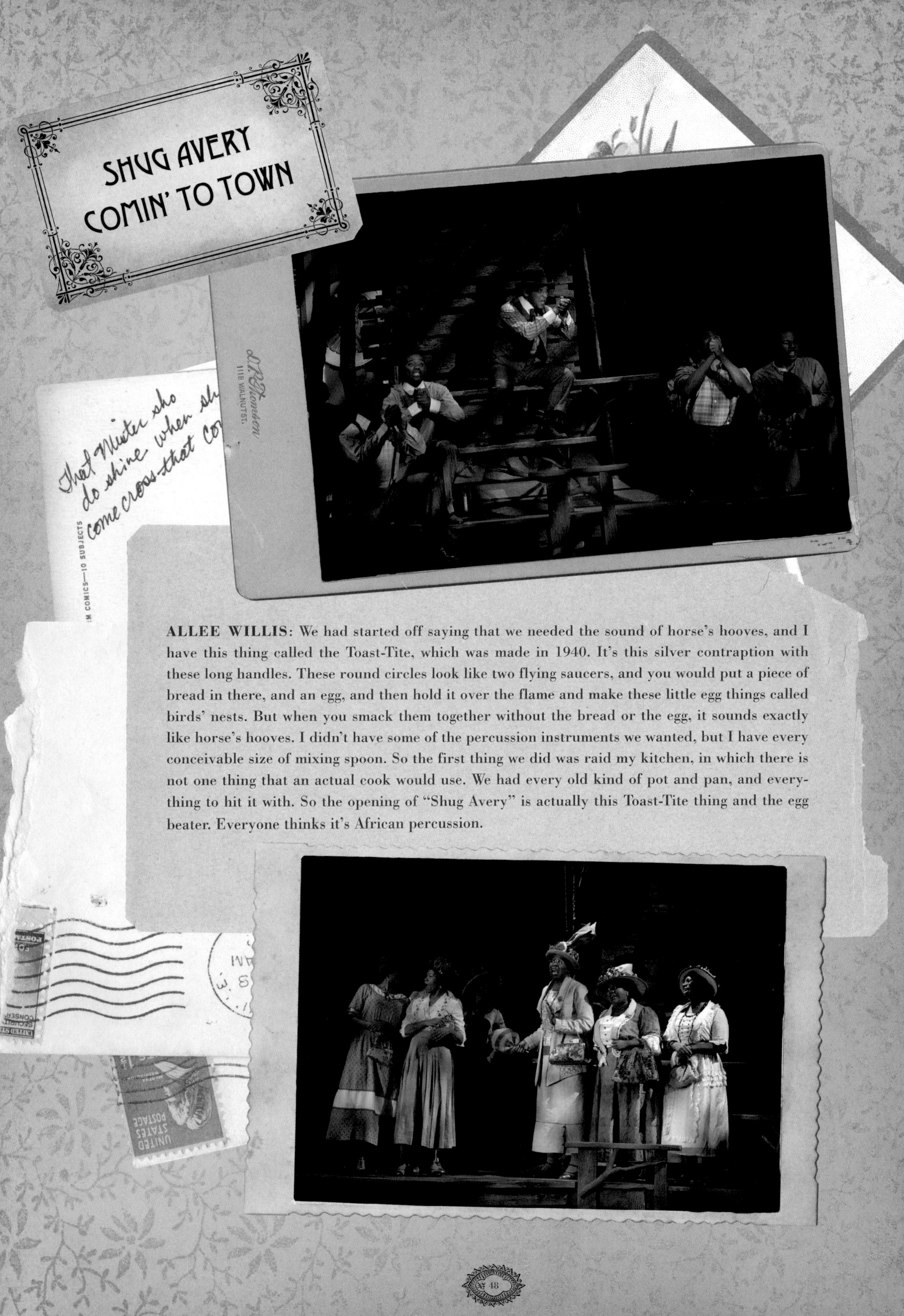

ALLEE WILLIS: We had started off saying that we needed the sound of horse's hooves, and I have this thing called the Toast-Tite, which was made in 1940. It's this silver contraption with these long handles. These round circles look like two flying saucers, and you would put a piece of bread in there, and an egg, and then hold it over the flame and make these little egg things called birds' nests. But when you smack them together without the bread or the egg, it sounds exactly like horse's hooves. I didn't have some of the percussion instruments we wanted, but I have every conceivable size of mixing spoon. So the first thing we did was raid my kitchen, in which there is not one thing that an actual cook would use. We had every old kind of pot and pan, and everything to hit it with. So the opening of "Shug Avery" is actually this Toast-Tite thing and the egg beater. Everyone thinks it's African percussion.

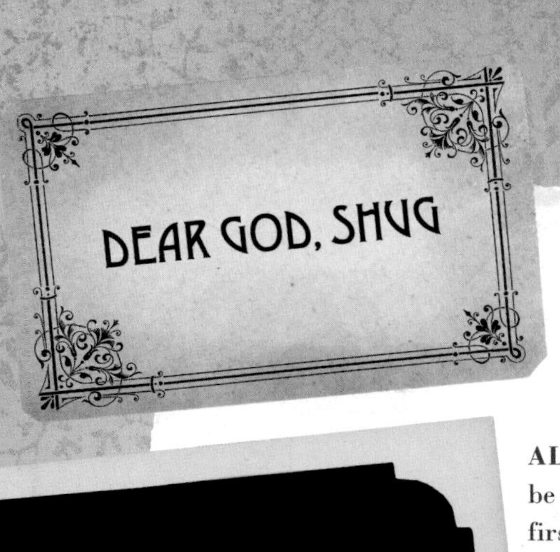

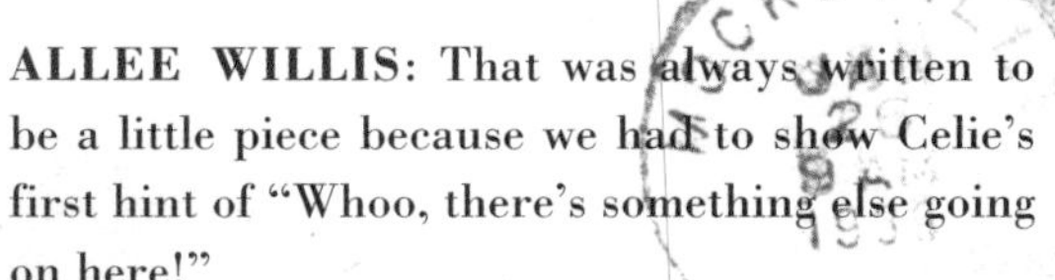

ALLEE WILLIS: That was always written to be a little piece because we had to show Celie's first hint of "Whoo, there's something else going on here!"

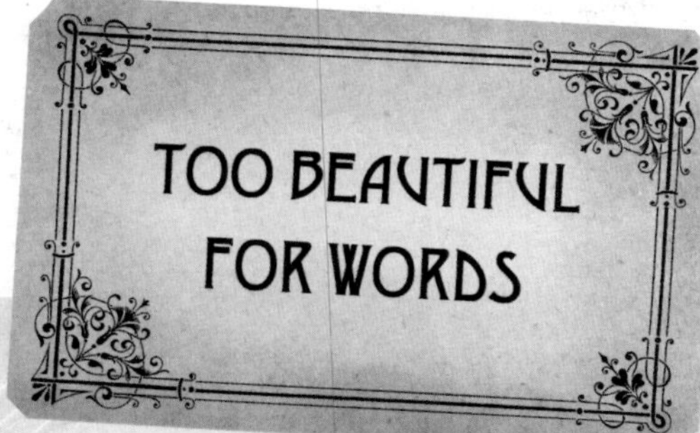

BRENDA RUSSELL: One of the prettiest songs we came up with in the show, I think. Melodically and everything. It was just a moving, short piece. And Elisabeth was born to play that part.

ALLEE WILLIS: "Too Beautiful" was maybe the seventh or eighth song we wrote, and we wanted a really simple song. At this point, we were still thinking about how the movie played that scene in the juke joint. It's the famous song called "Sister" from the movie that everyone asks to this day if it's still in the musical. But we felt Celie was this little wounded bird, and Shug really recognized that. Shug did see her beauty, because Celie was the first person who did anything for her without wanting anything, and so it shouldn't be the same kind of friendly, casual bluesy thing. It would be the deepest and most real that Shug had ever gotten with a song.

At first, Shug was going to sing "Push Da Button," and then she would quiet the crowd and say, "I wrote this song for Miss Celie, who combed it out of my head one day when I wasn't feeling good." We eventually took it out of the club because it would be more personal if it happened in the room between the two women.

BRENDA RUSSELL: We got that concept from Alice's book, of course, and we just wanted it to be a really raunchy, fun song for Shug, just to have a real good time.

BRENDA RUSSELL: I started playing that little rhythm thing that happens under "Uh Oh!" and we were hammering on that for a long time, and then I went to the ladies' room, and suddenly this whole other piece of music came to me. I came back and said, "I know we're working on this, but I got this other thing." We were never linear about anything. If something was coming through, you had to just say here it is. So I started saying this whole "His name is Henry, Henry Broadnax." I started playing that. I said, "I don't know what it is." And Allee said, "I know what it is," and she started to sing the melody and the lyrics, just started singing, "This here is Henry, Henry Broadnax." I was like, Yes!, and we inserted that right in the middle of what we were working on.

STEPHEN BRAY: Before Marsha Norman came into it, a lot of the scenes were fully musicalized. "Uh Oh!" was typical of them and is the only one that remains. But the confrontation when Sofia first meets Mister, all that dialogue is actually lyrics from the song that used to be there. There were four or five scenes we had written that were fully musicalized, and somehow "Uh Oh!" survived.

WHAT ABOUT LOVE?

STEPHEN BRAY: When were in Atlanta—the first time this song was performed in front of an audience—I heard a man down the aisle from me just burst out, "That's beautiful!" the first time he heard the chorus of that song. It just shot out of him like he couldn't help it. I loved that. Right after the song ended I saw a woman with tears coming down her face get up and go make a phone call, and we imagined, Somebody has made a life decision change based on that song. Something just became okay for this woman. I love that. I really do believe it does that to people. You would always hear the applause start slow, like, Let me look around and see if everyone's applauding this lesbian stuff. Is this okay? Sure enough, it started softly and got louder and then the whoops and whistles and everybody was totally into it. But it would always start off like, Hmmm, I don't know if it's okay if people see me clapping. So I just love that we were brave enough to have a lesbian love song, to put it on the stage and not shy away from it. I'm really proud of that.

ALLEE WILLIS: "What About Love?" was Scott coming to us in 2003, saying that as happy as he was that we were being pretty authentic, we needed to deal with the reality of the soundtrack. We needed a song that was going to sound like it belonged in the show, but that if you had to pick a song to go on the radio, this would be it. The three of us, coming from pop music, thought this was going to be a no-brainer, and it wasn't. It was hard because we had gotten this whole palette of instruments together, and it was just really hard to write something that could live in two worlds that happened to have been eighty years apart. How do you write for that? In the end we decided that the contemporary instruments we used would have to be held to a guitar, a piano—instruments that were in existence back then.

AFRICAN HOMELAND

ALLEE WILLIS: "African Homeland" is really important in that Celie discovers Nettie's alive and there. The whole spirit of the African people is exciting to Celie, but a lot of the stuff going on where Celie's living is also going on in Africa, and not just with the cultures, but with the men toward the women. So that was important to see. We knew we had to have it in, but it was really hard.

How do you show that this is in someone's imagination? In Atlanta we didn't have Nettie and Celie together, and there was something that was too impersonal about it. So that was an active discussion for a long time, how you had to see them together, you had to see Celie with the kids but somehow know she's still in Georgia, which is why Mister walks into the middle of it, and why Harpo walks through it.

And then there was layering in Sofia's story, because Sofia's story of getting beaten down parallels how the African people get beaten down; they're both forced to leave their homes.

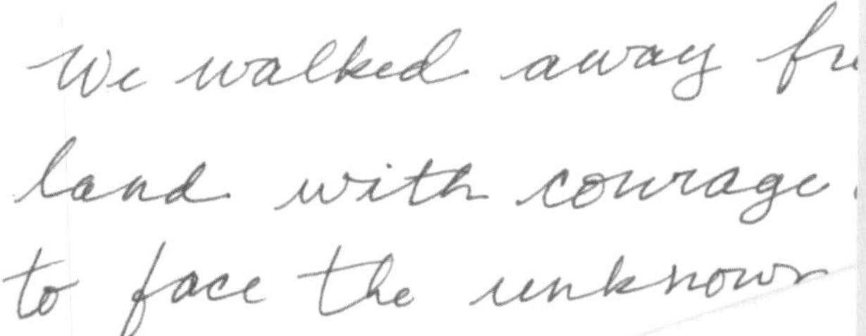

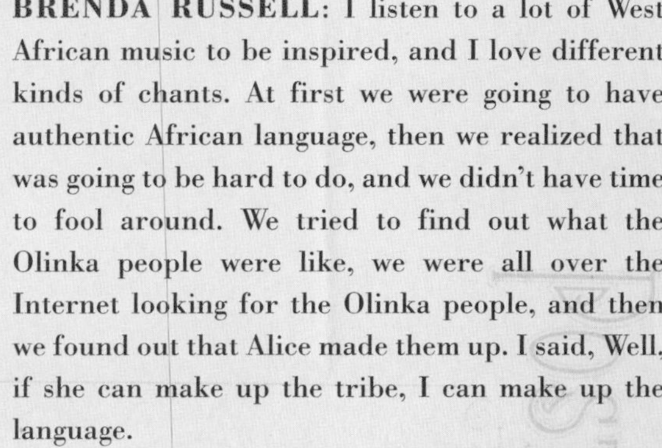

BRENDA RUSSELL: I listen to a lot of West African music to be inspired, and I love different kinds of chants. At first we were going to have authentic African language, then we realized that was going to be hard to do, and we didn't have time to fool around. We tried to find out what the Olinka people were like, we were all over the Internet looking for the Olinka people, and then we found out that Alice made them up. I said, Well, if she can make up the tribe, I can make up the language.

That, to me, was some of the most fun—writing the African music. We had a ball doing that and the percussion; we tried to be true to an authentic African sound. This is where American rhythms come from—the slave music evolving into gospel, into the blues, into R&B, into rock and roll, all of it. And a lot of that sound is based on the heartbeat. Bump-bump.

THE COLOR PURPLE

STEPHEN BRAY: We wrote the song for the end of the show, then we realized that Celie just can't sing that, she has to have gotten it from somewhere. We know that Shug showed her what was going on with the flowers and the trees and the waves and the ocean, so that first appearance of the song was born out of a need to have Shug's belief system presented to Celie at some point prior to Celie incorporating that into her own way of dealing with the world. We really wrote it for the end, and then realized we needed to give a glimpse of it earlier on.

BRENDA RUSSELL: "The Color Purple" was tricky to turn into a song, because it was the title of the show and we didn't want it to be corny. So as I'm sitting there, playing those changes and humming the melody, just trying so hard, digging so deep, Stephen there in the room and Allee there, and she's got the book, and she's walking around with these words, and then suddenly it seemed like, Oh, here it is. The whole energy in the room changed as soon as I found the right chord, started singing that melody, and then Allee was like, "Okay. I've got it," and she starts singing the words to what I was playing, and it was just magical.

ALLEE WILLIS: Brenda had some chords, she and Stephen started messing around with the melody, I picked up the book and thought, That's a brilliant melody, I think these words are going to work. On a tape I had made of that session, there's a part where I say something like, "All right, take a valium." I started singing, "Like a blade of corn, like a dah, dah, dah...." I was singing, "Like a dah, dah, dah, all a part of me, like the color purple, where do it come from? Now my eyes are open, look what God has done," and they just screamed. We kept screaming for maybe five minutes. It was by far the high point of the writing experience, because we never thought we'd get "The Color Purple" into anything. And no one ever asked us to, either.

Then I remember Stephen didn't like "Now my eyes are open, look what God has done," and we spent four days trying to get those last two lines. When we were completely exhausted, I tried one of my old faithful tricks, which was to pretend that I had just come up with it: "What about 'Now my eyes are open, look what God has done?'" and they said, "Oh my God, that's fantastic." Reading this is the first time they're going to realize they were taken.

CHURCH LADIES' EASTER

ALLEE WILLIS: Stephen pretty much had been the engineer on the road. He was the one who really knew the equipment. But he had to go to L.A., and we had to write this piece, so we couldn't wait for him to come back. We didn't get up to our hotel until maybe ten o'clock at night, and we were both dead. We didn't know how we were even going to get it down on tape, and it was just one of those moments where Brenda started playing those little string plucks, chink, chink, chink, and I literally started singing, "That's such a lovely hat, a fine chapeau." I don't even know where "chapeau" came from, because God knows none of those women ever studied French.

BRENDA RUSSELL: We decided that they were sort of the highfalutin' black ladies, so they would know a little French. It's not so far off because my great-grandmother studied French. They were not fooling around back in the day. They wanted to educate themselves, and they learned French, so it wasn't unheard of that rural Southern people would understand about French.

ALLEE WILLIS: We just laughed through that song, and then Stephen came back a couple days after and loved the piece. Brenda engineered that night and got us through, and that was one of those times where we didn't feel like we were steering the ship. We wrote that very quickly, and it puts me in a good mood every time I hear it.

I CURSE YOU MISTER

WM. BEATTY

DAISY
TENNESSEE STATE
FLOWER

STATE CAPITOL, NASHVILLE, TENN.

FOR CORRESPONDENCE FOR ADDRESS

STEPHEN BRAY: This is the first time Celie really says, You know what? Enough. She belts and she sings in a way she hasn't before. A lot of people said we had a lead who doesn't sing enough. But fortunately most of them were smart enough to say you've also got an abused, battered, shut-down, virtual slave of a person. So you can't have that person singing much unless you're going to have them singing "woe is me." It wasn't going to be that kind of dirge-like show. So that's why this is such a celebratory moment, when Celie finally says "enough" and belts it for all those within earshot to hear.

Series 108 H

MISTER'S SONG

CELIE'S CURSE

STEPHEN BRAY: There's an axiom that you don't write musicals, you rewrite them. When people were warning us what we were up for, they said you are going to be writing until the day you open. It was pretty much true. I think we stopped a couple of days before the first previews, and the last song we wrote was "Mister's Song."

BRENDA RUSSELL: A few days before the opening, we had a different version of it, something like the fifth rewrite, and Kingsley looked at us, and he said, "I'm not feeling it."

ALLEE WILLIS: What we had was a little too sentimental, and Mister's transformation happened too quickly. So we had one final massive pow-wow, talking about "it needs to say this, it needs to say that." Marsha was unbelievable in quite a few ways, but my favorite was that she was amazingly spontaneous and fearless. If you say, Give me some idea of what you're thinking, most people give a five-word synopsis. Marsha starts spouting out anything that comes to mind. I furiously wrote down whatever she said because I trusted her instincts. Here, she said, "No one in this town respects me, my father treated me like shit, my woman's sleeping with my wife…." We put in order what Marsha was saying and turned it into a lyric. We had maybe only a day before the critics came. This is not a medium for the faint-hearted. It put me to the test, and no one likes to walk a tightrope like me. But it was harrowing.

STEPHEN BRAY: I consider anyone who would behave as Mister did, to some degree, emotionally damaged. I'm not saying that people need not be punished and brought to justice for what they do. But I think it is important to understand why people do what they do if we're ever going to prevent it. So hopefully that song shows you that Mister is part of a patriarchal chain that insists on a kind of behavior for men that basically drives them crazy. This is a man whose passion was shut down and taken from him. His passion wasn't able to sustain his father's attempts to shut it down. That turns you bitter and makes you hard and cold and evil. You want people to suffer like you suffered. Then Harpo comes in the picture and says, "Hey, Pop. What's going on?" Mister sees Harpo, which makes him think, Wait a minute. I tried to do the same thing to Harpo that was done to me but it didn't work. Look at him. He's happy. His mama died in his arms. His wife left him. What right has he got to be happy? I don't know whether we achieve it or not but hopefully you see that Harpo's good comes from within and that his love for Sofia has just outshone all the darkness around him. Then Mister asks whether it's not going to be something he says that changes his life. Maybe it's going to be what he does that will bring his life into a better place. Hopefully we walk away wondering and hoping that he will.

MISS CELIE'S PANTS

BRENDA RUSSELL: "Who dat say, who dat say," was crawling around my head. I had this hook and these chords, and I realized this is going to be the '40s song we needed for Celie's pants song. I wrote it at home, recorded it, and brought it in on Allee's birthday. I said, "I have a great birthday present for you," and she is looking behind my back like, "Where is it?" I pulled out the disc and played it for her and Stephen. Initially I had to pull them in a little bit. They liked it musically, but at first they weren't sure about the "Who dat say" line. And I was very gung-ho about it.

ALLEE WILLIS: I loved it, but thought it was a little too directly the kind of music that would have been happening then. So we tried to write verses that would not have typically gone with that kind of melody. We wrote a song that everyone seemed to love, and when we got to Atlanta, no one liked the lyrics. They felt that it was more like a novelty song, because the song was about Celie's fantasy of how she was going to make all these different pairs of pants.

A little of that remains now, but not much. That was the first time we really had to deal with how you can't just have a song that seems to work for the moment. It's got to push the story. Not only do we need to learn about Celie, but also how does this push her to getting close to the epiphanic moment she has later in "I'm Here"? So that song went from being the easiest one to the nightmarish one. At one point in New York it was completely thrown out. We understood that you can't just have a feel-good song in the middle of everything, but it was so effective with the audiences, and it was so Celie's spirit, it just made sense to us. So we rewrote that lyric a good fifteen times.

MARSHA NORMAN (Book Writer): This is a song that I was really involved with. I said to them, We need a song for Harpo and Sofia. We need it to be really sexy. We need it to start out with work. It was one of those places where a book writer comes in and says, This is what we need right here. It's completely a scene that we are totally unprepared for: They start out fussing and end up sexed up and ready to go. This is what we need for them. And it needs to be about work. One thing I felt coming out of Atlanta was that we had to really play up and complete the story of how hard everybody works. It wasn't just that they were living in a drama; they were living in farms and fields and houses that demanded constant labor. So the construction of that song, that "is there anything I can do for you, anything else I can do for you," came out of the work and the passion.

STEPHEN BRAY: I can picture the hotel room at the Atlanta Marriott on Peachtree where that one came together. I can probably tell you the address. I can see us: We're in that room and Brenda is really sick and we're like, Okay, they need the song tomorrow. Gary and Marsha or someone would come and say, We need another song and we need it tomorrow. Often, those challenges would result in something that is now a favorite. But they needed something more from Harpo and Sofia that showed that they're the true love story. Harpo and Sofia are the ones who were in love from the beginning and they stay in love. They have their issues but they stay in love from the beginning to the end and so we wanted to show that in the second act. We did that song it in a couple of hours and Felicia and Brandon were fantastic the first time they sang it.

MARSHA NORMAN: The hardest parts are when you can't figure out what song you need. You know that you need a character to sing, but you don't know what the song is. In this show, the hardest ones were probably Celie's "I'm Here" and "Mister's Song." There are probably ten versions of that Celie song, and they're very different from each other. They're not ten versions of the same song; they're ten songs. It's hard to figure out what both sums up where you've gotten to and doesn't yet complete the evening. This is the number that the lead character sings when they finally come upon the big treasure only to realize they have just a little bit further to go. It's the moment where Indiana Jones finds the gold, but he still has to get out of the cave.

BRENDA RUSSELL: It turned out to be one of the hardest songs to write, and it was a very important song because it's Celie's main song in the show. LaChanze helped us a lot. I remember when we were trying to write the lyrics, she started telling us how she felt in that moment. She said, "I want to flirt with somebody, I want to do this, I want to do that." It's great when the actors can articulate how they feel at that moment, because they're the ones playing the part, and they know the character inside out.

ALLEE WILLIS: A lot of people outside of the music-writing team didn't feel it was appropriate to go to a statement like "Loving who I really am,"—that maybe Celie was being a little too aware of herself in a contemporary way.

STEPHEN BRAY: In the moment where she says, "Most of all, I'm thankful for knowing who I really am," I was accused of being a bit psychotherapy cheesy. But for me it totally works because, without it, you can't then say in the next breath, "I'm beautiful, Yes, I'm beautiful."

On some nights you can tell the people in the audience who are hearing that for the first time. They get a hint of it inside themselves and they go, That's me, I am beautiful. It's gut-wrenching to feel that in the audience when somebody next to you gets that. It is a story for everybody, but this is truly a women's moment because of what women are made to endure in terms of what beauty is, especially women who have not been called beautiful maybe just because they're black. I'll probably take that back at some point in the future when I really think about it because obviously men get to be beautiful too. When I grew up I went to an all-white school. I had the big lips and the wide nose and kinky hair and I was not considered beautiful. But in our culture men aren't concerned with being beautiful the way women have been tricked into feeling that if they're not outwardly beautiful, they don't really have what it takes.

ALLEE WILLIS: During previews was the first time we were going to hear this arrangement fully orchestrated and we were backstage, stuck up on the fifth floor. All of us were in the hallway stationed around this loudspeaker, and when she got to "I'm Beautiful," the audience burst into applause, and it was the first time ever that song went over the way we had heard it in our heads.

LOW PRESSURE CONDENSATE

Chapter Three

The Look

Paul Tazewell presents his sketches to the cast and creative tea

Making the costumes

PAUL TAZEWELL (Costume Designer): I heard through a friend who had heard on some obscure radio station that there were plans to do a musical of *The Color Purple*. This was probably two years before we actually did the production in Atlanta. I love the book, I love the movie. I remember reading the book when I was in high school. At the time, there were very few popular novels about the African-American experience, and it really spoke to me, just because it was a clear and creative telling of black experience. Anything that came after that, that involved *The Color Purple*, I was interested in.

Although there are some beautiful period costumes in the show, the draw for me was more than just making beautiful dresses. What's important is to clearly render who these people might be and to make them as individual as possible.

The range that was within the piece was a challenge: It goes through so many different periods, and it's rare that you see photographs that a black person might have of their ancestors. To get a photograph, you had to have money to have one taken. As you get closer to contemporary times, they're easier to find. So that search was one challenge, as well as putting in my two cents of how I viewed these people and rendering them with dignity so that it didn't become just about poor black people—each of them is a fully realized being.

GARY GRIFFIN (Director): In addition to being accurate, we thought a great deal of what the clothes had to reflect was pride. And how do these characters express their pride? Sometimes when you design costumes for this kind of play, you try to show they're poor, you try to show they're old. And the âudience goes, Okay, it's 1910 and they're poor. I didn't want to avoid that, but I wanted our focus to be how these people wanted to present themselves. When we choose clothes for ourselves, a sense of personal pride comes out. So I wanted to be sure that audiences responded to the characters' sense of themselves through the clothes.

PAUL TAZEWELL: One way dignity comes across is in the hats. African-American women took the idea of the turban or elaborate hairstyle—you actually see a made-up version of that in our Africa section—and made it important to how they see themselves and what they put out there in terms of beauty and style. So we follow through with the idea of the hat taking the place of the turban or headdress and then shifting and modulating to specific time periods.

Even if an African-American woman is poor, she does the best she can to look her best. Especially for Sunday. And absolutely for Easter Sunday. So there was a lot of care that went into the choices of what anybody would put on. I carry with me the memories of my grandmother and my great grandmother, so I've seen what style is and how it's carried through. I carry it through my daily life as well. When I walk into a store or a meeting, the first impression a person has of me is what I'm wearing. What I'm doing as a costume designer is trying to send messages as clearly as possible of who a person is and how that character might shift and open up as we get deeper into the story. There are many layers you can present in the immediate visual setup: What does the clothing look like? Are people poor or rich or somewhere in-between? Are they trying to act rich but have a pair of dusty shoes on?

How literal you are is a question of scale. If you were doing an opera and you have a large house, you have to bump up the size of your details, whether they're buttons or ribbons, in order for them to project to the back of the house. I'm trying to set up a look that is as natural and as true to the period as possible. For me, it's having all of those details, it's having texture, because that helps create a world that you can buy into, so you then trust that the story you're getting is also believable.

The original idea for Celie's pants is that they are pants that fit anyone. Given all the body types we have in the cast, the challenge was to make the actors look as good as sthey feel in them. Then, also, to have it look period, to draw from fabrics that Celie may have been able to find, things that she would think of as a home sewer and then translate that into this pants pattern.

She would look at a fashion magazine of the period and say, I'm going to try and use this style of lines. So we've got a pair of denim overalls that create a Rosie the Riveter quality because of the war that was going on at the time. Then there's a pair of pants that has an insertion of white into brown that seemed like an appropriate period color combination. It took my assistants quite a bit of going out and searching for fabrics, and me trying to patchwork things together and make it all cohesive.

I went with a full cut that could look good on all the body types we have because it falls directly from the

hip. If you look at the women who were wearing pants at the time, like Marlene Dietrich or Katharine Hepburn, it's more tailored, but still straight-cut full-legged pants.

When you put the designs into production, as much as you can, you want to be in one shop. You try and contain it. But the ballpark figure of how many costumes are in the show is around 260, 275. For any musical, it's a large cast. Because of the time pressure, we were producing costumes in somewhere between five and seven shops, if you include the milliner. We needed to split the clothes up because each shop could only take on a certain amount of work. We had one shop doing most of the dancers' things, one doing most of the singers', one doing most of the men's, and one shop doing our principal ladies. We had basically one shop doing all of our headgear, except for another craftsman who did all the African stuff and another craftsman who did some of the dancers...so it was divvied up all over as well as outside the city. The person who built some of the African headdresses is from Washington, D.C.

It was the job of my very talented associates to figure out the logistics. We needed the actors for as much time as we could have them, Gary wanted them for as much time as he could, and Donald wanted them for as much time as he could. If one shop is building most of an actor's clothing line, then you have to pull him or her out of rehearsal fewer times. In the end, it was kind of nutty figuring out how to see the cast as much as we needed to.

And the cast was fantastic. It was gratifying to me as a designer to have the clothes liked, and I would hear that over and over. Even from LaChanze, whose things are very humble against everybody else's because of her character. In a fitting, she would put this face on and shift her body, and it would be Celie. You would see that transformation in the mirror. To be a part of that is like nothing else because it feels like you are creating magic.

I become very moved when I know I've had a part in supporting the story. And then when you see the audience stand on their feet nightly and give the cast ovations, you realize, My God, some of what the audience is feeling is because of what I've brought to the stage.

"One way dignity comes across is in the hats"

—PAUL TAZEWELL

Felicia gets into costume

Fitting Shug

Trying on the dress for "Push Da Button"

Shug comes to town in a black dress

Shug's Easter suit

The dress Shug wears for "The Color Purple"

Chuck LaPointe works his magic on the Church Ladies

An Easter hat fitting

Some wigs required
pin curls each night

MARSHA NORMAN (Book Writer): He's a genius, Chuck [LaPointe, wig designer]. When people ask me how we accomplished the passage of time in the show, I say it's the wigs. The hair is the story of the people: That's a big way audiences can gauge how old everybody is and what has happened to them. And of course, what I learned in working with Stephen, and Brenda in particular, because Brenda's very hair-conscious, is that this is a thing. They said to me, "Look, black women think about their hair a lot; this is a big piece of communication." It was a real awakening for me.

CHARLES G. LAPOINTE (Wig Designer): Paul [Tazewell] and I met while working on *Raisin in the Sun*, and that's how I came to *The Color Purple*. He asked me to do it, and there I was in Atlanta with no money, trying to make this huge show work with very specific styles of hair.

At the beginning of the process, I had Paul's sketches. I looked them over, got a sense of where we were going, and then I met the actresses and did the head wraps, which is basically a plastic bag and tape. I put a plastic bag over their heads, they breathed deeply, and I taped them up. Then I put the bags on canvas blocks and stuffed them out so I actually had a replication of their heads. They had their hairlines, it had all the ins and outs of the shape of their heads, where their own hair would lie when it's wrapped up and prepped for the show. And from that I built a cap, which is of a very thin, super lace. For this show, I used a lot of stretch caps because the actors' heads were so big. Some of these girls have, in real life, twenty-two-inch heads, but with dreadlocks or hair extensions, they have twenty-five- to twenty-six-inch heads. There's a lot we had to do to cover up all that hair. In the end, it makes your job more difficult, because you're trying to create an illusion that this wig is actually their hair.

Once we had the cap, we took a barbed needle that's like a fishhook and used that to weave hair through the cap one hair at a time. It's called ventilating. In the back of the wig you're often using three and four hairs in a knot because you need it to be thicker back there. In the front, because you are simulating someone's actual hairline, you're using only one hair at a time.

There's only one wig that's synthetic; the rest are human hair. Because the wigs are natural hair, there isn't a lot of maintenance on them. They just need to be smoothed over or the fuzzies taken out. Or sometimes they're totally soaked down, because they're naturally curly, and we're reviving the curl. The 1920s and 1930s wigs need to be wet set, so they're soaked down, set in rollers, and then put in a wig dryer.

Initially, I was nervous about how I would be perceived being a white man coming into a very, very specific, black woman's territory. Quintessentially, black women's hair is the most important self-image issue they deal with. And when I had my first fitting with LaChanze, she just looked at me like, You've got to be kidding. I got it from day one. Walking in the door, she was looking at me like, How could this white guy have any idea? I was able to come through for her; it ended up never being a problem. In the end, like any actress, you are dealing with someone's own self-image coming into play. Knowing that, I had to let my instincts take over, because I didn't know black hair from anything else. I got caught so many times on the subway staring at black women's hair to see how it grew out of the head. I can't tell you the number of times women have looked at me like, What is the matter with you? What are you doing? That was really my research, along with looking at photos and talking to Paul. Oftentimes I would half-make a wig and then bring Paul in to see if I had the right idea. And then, truthfully, there were so many wigs in that show, about one hundred twenty, that in eight weeks, I had to just say, "Do it." We winged it, and it worked.

It seems to be something I do well, black hair. I don't know what it is, or why it is, but these girls have told me they're the best wigs they've ever worn. So I guess I found my calling. Part of it may be that my partner [Tom Watson] and I believe that the wigs have to look natural. There should never be a question that what's on the person's head isn't their hair. Where people often go wrong is in trying to overglamorize. In *The Color Purple*, we tried to keep it all very realistic. That's maybe what made a difference. And that they fit. These wigs were actually made for these girls. And some of them have five to wear. It made me weepy, actually, doing some of these final fittings, because the wigs would just simply lay down on their heads, almost as if suction was pulling that hair down to the scalp. And it became their hair. I had a couple of them cry, they were just so relieved. Because it's a big deal. It's a big deal for them.

John Lee Beatty's Set

Walking behind a set model

GARY GRIFFIN: The visuals were all designed around movement, in the sense of keeping things moving forward, following the show's progression. And so on almost every level, we talked about visual rhythm before we talked about look. For example, in six minutes' worth of text, you're going to start in the field and run to a house, be in the house and then the house is going to go away. That's what the text is saying. You don't want the audience to be exhausted by all that scenery moving around. That has to do more with rhythm than it has to do with look. When we figured that out, then we could talk about how those trees should look and what was Georgia. We wanted the set to have a lot of texture, to be sensual in the sense that you could feel the scenery.

JOHN LEE BEATTY (Set Designer): I had read the book years ago and loved it, and [when I was hired] I purposely didn't read it again. I wanted to make sure that what was on the stage was what was written for the stage, rather than leftovers that couldn't be understood without having read the book. We were not trying to invite people out of the experience; we were trying to invite people in. In fact, when we changed the scenery from Atlanta to Broadway, we kept trying for clarification rather than more confusion. We took out a casket, and we had one too many houses. Especially when you have characters named Mister and Pa, it got confusing about whose house we were talking about. Also, instead of Celie coming back to the tree as she does on Broadway, in Atlanta she came back to Pa's house where she was mistreated as a child. By her returning to the tree and the earth rather than to Pa's house, it cleaned up the storyline. Also, emotionally, I'd like to think Celie returning to her—I hate to say this—roots was a more valid metaphor. She's not looking forward to returning to the house she was abused in. She's actually looking forward to returning to herself and her childhood. So we made the tree a symbol of her childhood. It's not true to the book, but in a funny way, it's truer.

In terms of developing the show's aesthetic, first of all, one is confronted with the title of the piece, which is *The Color Purple*. I'm sure if you're an actor and the title is *Hamlet* and you're playing Hamlet, it's daunting. Well, if you're a designer and the title is the color, there's that problem, first of all. Obviously the metaphor of what *The Color Purple* means to people is built into it. We had to deal with that head on, and then try to forget it as we went along, because you can't worry about it all the time.

Before we even started in Atlanta, I visited the shop where we were going to build the sets. Behind the shop and over the garbage dump, there were some straggling trees in which a wisteria vine happened to be blooming. I took it as a good omen for the show, and you'll see that the vine actually is one of the final images—when Celie discovers the purple wisteria blooming on the trees. As we all know, LaChanze is actually an absolutely beautiful woman. Sometimes when you stand too close to her, you're astonished by how beautiful she is. One time we were in tech rehearsals in Atlanta, and she stood next to the wisteria and then turned and looked at it. Actually it was overwhelming to see her discovering the wisteria. Who was discovering it? I don't know if it was Celie or LaChanze or both. But I saw it happen. It was magical.

Along the way, people helped me find ways of getting purple in without getting caught. As we finished each piece of scenery, I would look at the painter and say, "Can you think of any problem we could solve by adding purple?" We would hide it in the corners, just a little bit of purple. Oddly, purple isn't my favorite color. I respect purple, but it hasn't always been my favorite. It's one of those weird colors: You can add it to a color like yellow, which is its complement, and it does very interesting things. I bet Alice Walker knew that about purple, that it's a strange color to add to a mix, because it has a curious calming effect as well as an exciting effect.

Because the musical moves like a house on fire, you couldn't do complicated movement that would stop the show. That was the hardest part to organize. We have things that slide and things that fly in and things that revolve and things that get out of the way of each other. The main thing to do is to make sure that whatever is there doesn't have to get out of the way before the next piece comes in. In Atlanta, we actually put the upstairs of Mister's house upstairs and the downstairs downstairs. It got very complicated, and we got hung up on the logistics of Celie going down and then going back up. When we decided we'd pretend that we were upstairs, it really loosened up the whole show. That also meant we could worry less about the house and more about the story. It's sort of like the Clinton thing, "It's the economy, stupid." It's the story, stupid—Gary and I would say that to each other as we were working on it. We needed to keep our eye on Celie and the story and

Working on the tree

Celie's relationship to God, which is really the center of everything. In Atlanta, we didn't have the passerelle, which is the runway around the orchestra and the gangplank that comes down the center. And I really, really, really wanted for Celie to come forward and talk to God. We realized early on that her relationship to God is as important as it is to anybody else on stage.

To find images for the show, I went first to the obvious places, like Walker Evans's pictures of the South. I discarded those pretty fast, because, first of all, they're not in color. Second, I had a sense that they weren't what this really is about. It's deeper than that. Not that they're superficial, but it isn't a documentary. Instead, I started looking at contemporary African sculpture and African art. At the same time, I was looking at pictures of trees and at trees in general. It's weird how these things come together. The African and the American in this play are in some ways united. It's no secret that the planking on the proscenium is slightly reminiscent of a slave ship. So there's a connection between Africa, the ship, the United States, and the arc of these people's experiences. I felt that there was Africa in everything: that was one of the takeoff points. I also looked at the book *The Quilts of Gee's Bend.* Believe it or not, reading the book was as important to me as looking at the pictures. One of the woman quilter's lives is so similar to Celie's that it's frightening.

In *The Color Purple* set creation, the Africa section has always been a world unto itself. The freeing thing is when you realize, of course, it's Celie's vision. Again, it's not a documentary about Africa, nor is it *The Lion King*. It's this particular woman's vision of Africa. But she's got a feeling, and I've got to believe, deep in Celie, she knows what Africa looks like in her heart. I'm Scottish, English, and German, and when I went to Scotland, I thought, Hmmm, I've got a feeling. I think I've been here.

The African scenery was the last thing to join the show. The big sculptures, the snaky river twigs, came out of looking at African sculpture. Those are actually made of real plants intertwined with some hidden metal. But they're pretty natural, and I actually had the painters put mud on them.

Organic as one wants it to be, there's a lot of metal and plastic and a little bit of computer work in there. But the wonderful thing about scenery and the reason it's expensive is that this was not a machine-made product. Human hands are all over this with paintbrushes and sculpture. Even the steel was hand-welded. Making that tree involved two welders and carpenters and maybe five artists, painters, and sculptors at the same time. You're flying on the trust of this whole group while working under the gun.

Broadway's set was thrown together so quickly. We were doing a workshop, and all of the sudden, "You're going to Broadway, honey!" The lighting designer, Brian MacDevitt, and I were working together on a show at the time. We were out in Minneapolis and he came to me and said, "John, I have good news and I have bad news."

I said, "What is it?" He said, "Well, it's the same news. We're going to Broadway with *The Color Purple*." We were blessed that the theater opened up and was in immaculate shape, so it didn't need repairs. All the scenery was built in about a month. You'd turn around and there would be Africa on Mister's porch. Africa and the store would arrive on the same day. After it was all over, the stage manager and producer and I looked at each other and said, "Wow, nothing went wrong here. That's amazing."

The tree is a collage of splintered wood, roots and rope

JOHN LEE BEATTY'S

Sketches of the Set

This set is from the soul. It's not calculated, not a window dressing approach of making it pretty pretty to sell tickets. It just isn't that. And I guess one could have done more of a picture-postcard version of everything. But this is very handmade."

The backdrop has a transparent netting with plants on it. For technical reasons, we actually made them out of feathers that we gunked up with glue and starch. I wanted to get as many natural materials in as ever, and also it also gives it an odd sort depth, and you don't quite know what you're looking at. Is it lighting or projections or scenery or what?

—JOHN LEE BEATTY

Brian MacDevitt's Lighting Design

BRIAN MACDEVITT (Lighting Designer): I knew the film first and I don't normally think translating film to musical is successful. I always feel like, Let's leave it in its best genre and find something else to musicalize. But once I saw the direction the play was taking, I thought, This is my favorite thing to do, rather than doing a musical where you do "numbers" with flashing lights—a Vegas kind of thing we call "flash and trash." That's where the lighting is creating excitement, and unfortunately many times you're asked to do that because whatever's on stage isn't exciting enough. Even in Shug's juke joint number, we still want to keep honest to the space it's in. Having said that, it's all still within the world of musical theater: It's not a real place. The tree is a collage of splintered wood and roots and rope. When the curtain goes up, there's a big orange and purple sky that silhouettes the girls in the tree. But every color we use in the show can appear in nature, whereas in a flashy show, you might use a lot of neon, which is unnatural but exciting to the eye. At the same time it needs to be special, so it is filled with those once-in-a-lifetime skies you see if you have the patience and wherewithal at that time to take it in. There were times where we wanted to counterpoint the harshness and cruelty of the story with something beautiful. I would hope that makes the cruelty stand out even more, but I don't think anybody stops and thinks about it. I hope it's more subversive than that.

Africa is the one place where the colors are surreal, red juxtaposed with green, very bold, unnatural colors. It was inspired by indigenous African painters, and we used shocking, Fauvist, primary colors. The reason why is because if we set up a heightened sense of "reality" to begin with, then where do we go for the fantasy of Africa? What does Celie imagine this place is like?

I want these bold colors, but I never want it to look like there's red light. I want it to look like the landscape has turned red. I didn't want rock-and-roll lighting, where you put haze in the sky and see beams of colored light. I'm always troubled by that in the theater, because I don't want things to look like a rock concert.

Normally you'd think, Let's put all the lights on the actors. But what we also have is an army of lights in the stage floor that are just designated to do the sky from behind. That's what gives it that sense of infinite depth. If you projected sky from the audience side, you would see everybody's shadow projected onto something.

Everything about that light deck was especially designed for this show. In the wisdom of John Lee Beatty and Gary Griffin, they knew what benefit this show would have by assigning that space to lighting and to sky.

We decided there would be one time in the show that we would really use purple. We kept saying, we can't be living in the title through the whole show. At the very end of "I'm Here," there's a fleeting moment, maybe three seconds, where we zoom in to Celie, and the whole world turns this rich purple. I don't expect people to say, "Oh, purple!" I felt we should be smarter than to put her in a purple world. There are hints of purple throughout. At the very top of the show there's purple, and during Shug's "Color Purple" there is essence of purple in that. But at the end of "I'm Here," we go full on. We also sneak a little shooting star in there. I'm on the edge about that; I don't want to take people's attention away from the actors and have them say, "Oh, cool, look at what the light man's doing."

We always wanted to run the gamut, to find a way to go from the cruelest, angriest, most hurtful part of nature, to the most sublime and blissful. We talked about finding a place in the show where we could do an electrical storm and rain. We did it in Atlanta in one transition, and then it occurred to Gary that when Mister hits his lowest of lows, it's like a fever dream. So we decided that would be a good place to have thunder, lightning, rain—just really a crucible for him. To make the storm, we projected lightning bolts first on the back of the drop, and then we go right to this electrical storm. Mister comes out of the house like he's been driven out by bats and spirits, and he's half crazy from drinking. In about fifteen seconds the lightning travels from the sky to the house, and then right in front of him. The idea is that the electrical storm is from nature, but it's also part of his catharsis; that somehow out of that fever and the destruction of the storm grows his newfound love for himself, and by extension for the world around him.

It's funny because the designs that get recognized and awarded are usually things that wow you, and for designers and directors, their best work is usually in shows where the actors and the playwright gets the credit.

One other thing that deeply attracted me to this story—especially in these times—is that the God of the story is in nature. That, to me, is a universal truth that

all religions and human beings can share. What John Lee [Beatty] designed in the set enabled me to embrace beautiful skies. Throughout the show we surrounded Celie with beauty, and her journey was that she was so beat up she couldn't get outside of her pain to experience that beauty, which to me, is experiencing God. I'm deeply suspicious of organized religion. I feel like people take "God" and use that idea to oppress and judge other people. *The Color Purple* world is one that loves everybody, that just feels completely universal. It's the world I'd like to think I live in—I can experience the same beautiful skies that somebody in Iraq can experience. Celie finally gets to the point where Shug shows her: "Look around you. God made purple flowers, and it's a sin not to be in awe of that."

Even as a fallen Catholic, I still have some belief in God and magic, and that this has been a blessed project from the start. There's a power to the story; there's no vanity in this show because the story is bigger than any one person. At the same time, everybody works as hard as they can to serve it, as opposed to asking, "What kind of review am I going to get?" If there's an insecurity about what you're putting up there, people get desperate and graspy. If a ship gets leaky, people blame each other. This song doesn't work because it's not loud enough, it's not bright enough, the drums aren't right, the music's wrong, the staging's wrong, the costumes are wrong. If she were in a pink dress it would be funnier. If a ship gets leaky, it brings out the worst in people, and this has been airtight all along.

Testing the lights

Donald Byrd's Choreography

Choreographing the song "Uh Oh"

DONALD BYRD (Choreographer): I came on board after the Atlanta run. They were looking for a choreographer, and when I saw the show at the Alliance, I actually thought I was the ideal person to do it. I said, Okay, this is the show for me. I've always been really interested in African-American vernacular dancing and how you take that and heighten it so you can do it on a stage. I also felt I was right for the project because I grew up in the South and culturally, not just as an African-American but in terms of understanding the sensibilities of people in the South, it made sense to me and spoke to me.

I had wanted to do a Broadway show, but I felt my sensibility was a very particular one and wasn't suited for many things done on Broadway. But this show wasn't a musical comedy, the subject matter was intriguing, to say the least, and challenging for audiences. To find a way of translating that story into a musical theater piece was a big challenge and one worth pursuing.

I've always tried to incorporate vernacular and social dances into what I was doing. Like in the juke joint, some of the dances are based on dances that were done in the teens and early 1920s. They were called animal dances like the Buzzard Hop and the Bear Hug. Some of those were transformed later by Vernon and Irene Castle and became dances like the Foxtrot and the Castle Walk or the Continental. They were originally dances that were done in juke joints and they were close contact, highly sexualized dances.

Other dances are ways of moving I remember seeing people do as I was growing up. The men's dance in "Shug Avery Comin' to Town" is one of those and it kind of uses a suggestion of dances from the Motown era, like background dances the Four Tops and the Temptations would do, which were actually based on a way of moving from a generation before.

Movements, sensibilities, and tastes change. There are actually things in that particular section that look hip-hoppish. But those movements existed before hip-hop; now they're just attacked differently. With hip-hop, you place the accents differently. The way dances look to us now versus the way they looked thirty or forty years ago is that things are just faster. They're more percussive and they're more aggressive. So, if you really want to get a sense of what they looked like before, you slow them down and take some of the movement out so there's less visual information that you're giving an audience.

When we got to Africa, the concern I had was how to not have it be authentic. I wanted something that felt like authentic African dance but was not real African dance because it's happening in Celie's mind; that she's visualizing, she's imagining what Africa might be like from reading the letters from her sister. Some of what the dancers do near the beginning is very small and exotic-looking movement, and that is based more on dances from Bali and from Indonesia. So their costuming is Africanized, but the movement really does not fit with what you think African movement is. There are a few steps that are real authentic West African dance steps, but for the most part they're all inventions. We're looking at a fantasy. We're not looking at a real place.

One of the things Celie's struck by is that the people have dignity and that they have a certain level of agency in terms of how they participate in their society, that it is beautiful, it's colorful. It is complex and that the vitality of the community is communicated through the athleticism of the people in the community. So that was really what I was trying to do; that the movement's vitality and the acrobatic nature of it and the vigorousness of it is a metaphor for the community's vitality.

I like athletic, intelligent dancers. All the dancers in our show are smart and imaginative and capable of making choices. They take direction well, but they have incredible physical instruments, as well. That's really it. They're extraordinarily gifted physically. They do it and they make it look easy.

We knew that Africa was in her imagination, but I started to articulate it in a way that I think made sense to the director and to Marsha Norman, the book writer. One thing I said to them was we have to look at how the dancing becomes another element of the storytelling, and that the top of the second act has to look really different than the first act. They agreed with that. Obviously, in something as collaborative as Broadway, nothing hits the stage unless there is some consensus about it, especially the director and the book writer and the producers. And so they liked that solution that I had come up with, and they were very encouraging. And even when things weren't working, Gary Griffin would say, "Well, Donald's given us a lot, so now our job is to figure out how that really works into the complete context of the show."

The costumes, wigs, lighting, and set design all comes together for "Push Da Button"

Chapter Four

The Cast

Shug Avery and Celie

Sofia

The Rehearsals

BERNARD TELSEY (Casting Director): Ultimately, casting the show is the creative team's decision. It's our job to inform them as best we can about someone's talent outside of a ten-minute audition that could go one way or another. When it's cast and goes into rehearsal, countless creative members, from press to designers, start to work. Then we're gone.

For *Purple*, we were looking for an entire cast of African-Americans, which was wonderful and exciting, a way to introduce new talent and people who don't always get to be seen. *The Color Purple* specifically had so many women's roles—usually you have to say things like, She's not right because they don't want somebody skinny. In this particular case, if you were an African-American woman, there was at least one role you could be right for.

We initially pursued the idea of having a star list, from P. Diddy to Des'ree, but once the material got stronger Scott [Sanders] rightly said, "The piece is the star; we don't need that." I love Scott for coming to that conclusion, because what's wonderful is that Felicia [P. Fields] and Elisabeth [Withers-Mendes] and Renée [Elise Goldsberry], all of these people are getting their lead role breaks.

GARY GRIFFIN (Director): A lot of people would come to auditions and they would sing the song fine and clearly could act. But among the ones who ended up in our show, there was a visceral connection with the character—a level of personal attachment—that made you trust them as an audience. That's who I try to be when I'm auditioning. As much as I'm a director looking at skill, I try to also be an audience member. How do I respond as an audience member to watching this person inhabit this role?

Celie

One of my own little affirmations I used to say is that we're all different: A rose cannot be a daisy; it has to be a rose. So you have to be the best rose or daisy or tulip that you can be. I may be a daisy, but I am going to be the most beautiful daisy you've ever seen.

—LaChanze

GARY GRIFFIN: If you met LaChanze, you would not think she and Celie have a lot in common. LaChanze is outgoing and she's got this winning personality. But underneath Celie is a LaChanze. There's this strong will in Celie that has to be formed and shaped; Celie finds the power of her spirit over the course of this piece.

LACHANZE (Celie): Celie's journey is so clear to me—I have never had to "work" to generate the emotions of this character. It's visceral for me. Because of that, I am always transported to this character, every time I get on stage. Still, it's a draining role, emotionally. At times I don't want to do it; I just don't want to be Celie. Some days the weight of knowing that I have to be her is pretty heavy on me, because in order to do it right I have to commit in a way that makes me go through the journey she goes through eight times a week. The audience is engrossed and moved, and then they go home and get back into their lives with this feeling of being transformed by this thing we've done on stage. But the next day, I have to go back into this character.

At the same time, I absolutely love investigating her, finding humor in certain areas, finding joy, finding the different layers of Celie's personality.

My own favorite moment in the show is when Shug sings "Too Beautiful for Words" to Celie. That, and "I'm Here," when Celie decides to love herself, because there are so many people in the world who don't. The songs are similar in that they confirm self-love and acceptance. In one, this woman is saying to Celie, "You are something special. Believe it. I see it, I see it all over you," even though Celie doesn't get it then. In another scene she does get it and sings, "I'm Here." Both of those moments for me are special because they confirm that no matter what you feel like, this is who you are. It's a powerful message, and it's important. Once you believe that about yourself, not in a conceited way but a truthful way, so much changes. You're not depressed, you're not insecure, you're not afraid, you're not lonely; so many of those negative emotions are shed when you start to truly believe that you matter. We love people like that, don't we? They're the confident ones who walk through life without fear. We're blown away by them. That's because we want that for ourselves, and that's what I love about that moment in the show.

Another great moment is when Celie gets her first letter from Nettie. That is so shocking for me as the actor, because I'm not there. I am in this moment of feeling loved and beautiful and sensual for the first time ever with Shug. When she says she has something for me, my mind isn't anywhere near Nettie, and it's sort of a double whammy. I am being loved, and I have my ultimate memory of love.

CELIE AGES FORTY YEARS IN THE SHOW

AGING

Celie

To go from fourteen to almost sixty on stage, there are no tricks, there's no time for make-up, there's no time to do anything other than transform before your eyes. The only tools I have are my body and my voice and, as my instrument, my face, my expressions. To give the audience the belief that I am a fourteen year old, I take on the posture of a young girl. Young girls are very open and not aware of their bodies in the way that older women are, and they oftentimes are not standing up straight. Sometimes their heads are off to the side or they may have one hand up scratching the back of their head in insecurity, or they may twirl their hair, or they may look up off to the left but, it's just that they're not as aware of themselves. They're trying to communicate, they're trying to think, and they think with their bodies at times. As we get older, we become more aware of our bodies, and put our arms down and we stand stiller, and if we're an insecure woman, our heads are lower. If we are afraid of getting hit, as in Celie's case, we sort of have a little bit of a prepared sort of state we're in for being defensive—a hunched over shrug at all times that communicates fear.

As she ages, she walks like she has a bit of a—I wouldn't say limp, but her gait is not a straight, even gait. She leans to the right because that's the side she's used to prevent from getting hit on. I change my voice, also to help with the aging. When she's young, I made her voice have a raspy quality, because she doesn't really use her voice much and when you don't use your voice much, it's not clear all the time. And over time it got worse. It got lower and lower. My character's on stage the whole time. I set the tone for the time change, and if I am not changing, you don't believe that anyone else is going to change.

By the time Celie gets to the pants store scene, she's feeling more confident. At that point she's actually imitating women like Sofia. Sofia is her example of strength. When Celie's with Shug, she's the most comfortable, because she's feeling loved, and she is feeling beautiful. So she's a little bit more comfortable in her body. But she really does not feel herself until Shug leaves her. That's when she really says, I'm going to put my head up, I'm going to do this. I'm not going to do it because you told me; I'm not going to do it because you showed me. I'm going to do it because I believe that I am beautiful. That's when she really starts to walk evenly. That's when I decided that her shoulders would not be up anymore; her shoulders are down, relaxed, from that point on.

Sofia

I believe people should do what they enjoy doing. There was a time I was working in an office; it was horrible. I couldn't be an accountant. What I do with numbers, no one would want me to do. You have to find what you excel at. There have been many days when I was broke. I'd say Felicia, you're raising kids, you got to find a real job. You've been out of work a month, two months and then something would happen, maybe a commercial, a little something saying Not yet. Just hold on.

—FELICIA P. FIELDS

GARY GRIFFIN: Felicia is a force of nature. And it takes that kind of expansive personality to play this role, and really, the show's life depends on Sofia. We take you to some dark areas, and the hope that Sofia will return is a nice thing to have. As with all the principal characters, we see Sofia triumph. And we see her at rock bottom. When we show you the jail scene in which Sofia's at her lowest, you need to have enough emotional investment in her for that scene to land.

FELICIA P. FIELDS (Sofia): Years ago, Gary Griffin and I were doing *Carousel* in Chicago. They made me look like Oprah coming through the field in the movie, and so when I came onstage, I said, "You told Harpo to beat me?" Gary said, "Well, if I ever do the musical *The Color Purple*, I already have Sofia!" Not long after that, he called and said he had been hired to do this project.

I really am similar to the character. It's not a stretch. Because if a man tried to hit me, it's like, It ain't goin' on. I'm not shy or demure, just like the character of Sofia, which gets her in a lot of trouble. Now, mine has never gotten me in the trouble hers has gotten her in. But I've raised children, and Sofia has done the same. I've raised them by myself, and she's done the same.

Sofia is opinionated; she is strength. She is a foundation not to be moved. She's controlling; she knows she's cocky. When she comes into the juke joint, she's got a plan. There's a little pretty girl that Harpo's been messing around with, but men want strength. And that is Sofia. That's Shug. We're talking about trying to build Celie's confidence by putting these women in front of her to show her what can happen.

The producers of this show looked long and hard for all kinds of people. They could have easily gone with name people. But the wisdom in their decision is that you're not just coming to see Sidney Poitier, so you won't be disappointed if he's not here. You also don't come in with a preconceived notion about what each actor's body of work is, you don't have anything to compare it to. When I'm in Chicago, everybody knows my work, but here, the joy I have is in knowing my applause at the end of the night comes from nothing but my work on that stage. Nobody gave it to me. I earned what I get at the end of the night. That's the best feeling in the world.

Mister

I love the baby we all birthed, and I look forward to watching it grow old. I can't wait to come one day and watch somebody else be Mist That is why you want to create a role: You live forever. Whoever comes after us, we are going to live inside of those people, to some degree. Because this was created on our bodies and our rhythms, our vocal patterns,

—KINGSLEY LEGGS

GARY GRIFFIN: Mister's behavior is not acceptable, but if we don't understand his pain, then it becomes melodrama. And it was very important to me that it was more psychologically complex than that. I think Kingsley and everybody worked together to make sure that no matter how you felt about Mister, he was a human being. He wasn't just a symbol of brutality.

MARSHA NORMAN (Book Writer): Kingsley does the hard labor of holding the show together. He's the force everybody has to react against in the beginning. He has such power that when he brutalizes Celie and drives Nettie away, basically he creates the plot. Then he has this love for Shug that he has to deal with. Mister comes to personify all of the things Celie has to break away from. And yet she does this without hating him. "I don't hate you," she says at the end, which is this incredible lesson about how not hating him is what's allowed her to survive. Celie would go right down the drain if she were to get lost in this hatred for him. Ultimately, she doesn't, and he pulls out of that self that was ordained by earlier generations. We wanted to give Mister his full journey, all the way through to redemption.

KINGSLEY LEGGS (Mister): Creating a role is a wonderful thing as an actor. In the theater world, you spend most of your time trying to redefine something someone else created.

What is this man about? Well, he's abusive. So, that's about power. He's just making the choices he thinks are right. Because that's how he knows life to be. It's no different from Celie allowing herself to be abused. That's her truth, to be put upon. She can't imagine standing up for herself. That doesn't make her a bad person. It makes her do a lot of things that aren't to her advantage. But it's not viewed the same way as Mister, because it's passive.

Certainly, I do not condone abusive behavior in any form. But I don't think that Mister is so different from any human being. He's just a man, trying to live life the best he knows how with what he was given. We all have a lineage of what we get from our parents and our experiences. This is what he got, and he did the best with it that he could. When he saw something new, he had the courage to change.

This is the most sensitive work I've ever had to do. Because you have to get it so that it lands just right, so that they hate you just enough and yet are able to at the end go, Okay.

Shug Avery

I have a regular feeding schedule for my daughter in the morning and during the day we record. Then I come and do this at night, and the next day we start all over again. It's a lot. But I always tell my husband this: I say, you will never hear me complain because these are the days we pray for, that you can do music during the day, have a beautiful healthy family, and then come work with an amazing cast.

—ELISABETH WITHERS-MENDES

GARY GRIFFIN: My sense of Shug was of a person who has endured a lot. When we first see her, she's at a point where she's ill, and the strain of her life has taken a lot out of her. But we watch Celie bring Shug back to life, and Shug, she really rethinks her spirit. Celie sees that resilience and realizes that you can work your way back from a lot of pain.

BERNARD TELSEY: Elisabeth looked it, she sang it, and she had the attitude, in the best sense, of Shug. She had never been on stage before as an actor. But there are some times you just say, You know what? That's what a rehearsal process is for. That's what directing is for, and now get the rest of the creative team on it, and we'll make Elisabeth into somebody great.

ELISABETH WITHERS-MENDES (Shug): Shug is confident. Shug is proud. Shug does not take crap. Shug reads through B.S., and she calls it out when she sees it. Shug is honest. Shug is an opportunist. Shug is sassy. Shug is sexy. Shug loves love. Shug loves Celie. Shug loves Albert. Shug loves Sofia. Shug loves God. Shug loves drinking. Shug loves hanging out. Shug loves a good time. Shug wants you to feel good about yourself. and she doesn't have any time for self-pity and feeling bad and woe is me. She's like, Come on, let's keep it moving. Love yourself, let's keep it moving. Anything that has life, Shug loves.

I did go up to Gary just before previews, when it finally dawned on me that this is not like performing my songs in a stadium or at a club. Wait. These people are depending on me to do the same thing every night. It's not going to happen. So I went to Gary, and I said, "Gary, listen. I can't do this. I forgot to tell you, I can't do this." Everything is cued and I'm asking questions like, "What do you mean, a light cue?" I pulled Gary aside downstairs in the Broadway Theatre, way, way downstairs, and I said, "I can't do this. How do you keep it fresh?" And he gave me the best advice I've gotten, which was, "Elisabeth, you stand with your palms faced out when you're speaking to any actor on the stage, and it totally leaves you open."

When you're onstage and you keep yourself open, you listen. And when you really listen to someone, every night is going to be different. And to put a cap on that was what LaChanze said to me recently. She said, "Elisabeth, one of the most refreshing things about our time here with *The Color Purple* is working with you, because every night it's different. You're willing to take chances onstage; it's like you're really listening to me."

Harpo

"For me what the show also did was create friendships and relationships I will have for the rest of my life.
Again, maybe that is the thing about this show. It unites people. It brings people together."

—BRANDON VICTOR DIXON

GARY GRIFFIN: Harpo was a hard role to cast because of the aging he goes through. He starts as a young man and has to get into his forties. So that's difficult. And he really must be believable as a young man, and we had a lot of older guys who you just couldn't believe in the early phase of the role. Brandon came along and really had it all. Harpo's the hope for the males in the story; I think Brandon embodies that himself. And I happen to love the way he and Kingsley play as father and son, because I think there's something in their own relationship that works well that way. But Harpo is a tricky part because you have to believe he loves Sofia, and through everything he goes through with Squeak, you have to spend the evening hoping he and Sofia are going to figure it out. What makes that so tricky is once abuse comes into the story: He tries to hit her and she leaves him. But we need to believe this is someone who deserves to be forgiven.

BRANDON VICTOR DIXON (Harpo): I watched the movie before I went in for my first audition, and I cried throughout most of it. I sat there thinking, I'm gonna need a good twenty to thirty minutes of happiness at the end for me to feel like this can fly, because nobody wants to see a sad musical.

The movie, which is what most people are familiar with, gives a one-dimensional view of the males in this society. If you read the book, all these characters are fleshed out fully. They all live lives and go through a world that's turning and changing. And not only in terms of racial tensions in the society, but the roles of men and women and how our circumstances put pressure on us to act in certain ways.

Something people definitely need to remember is that it's not an indictment of men in general, nor is it an indictment of black men. The men are people doing the best they can. It's important to understand that as a man coming to see this show, you won't feel attacked. You will ultimately feel liberated.

"Any Little Thing" is a favorite part because of my relationship with Felicia [Sofia]. That number has been generally structured, but Gary gave us the freedom to do what we want. We get to go out there and just play. We hit strides where we do the same thing, but I think the audience responds so highly to it every time because they see we're enjoying each other.

Nettie

In a very dark world, at the same time Celie's making decisions that are bad for herself on Nettie's behalf, Nettie has to be Celie's light. For me, it was the easiest thing in the world. I just fell in love with who Celie is and I fell in love with LaChanze. The rest was just like walking and talking. That's really it.

—RENÉE ELISE GOLDSBERRY

GARY GRIFFIN: Nettie was a terribly difficult role to cast, for very special reasons. She is a human embodiment of the hope that kept Celie going.

RENÉE ELISE GOLDSBERRY (Original Nettie): I want to celebrate the decision that Scott and the creative team made to hire me, knowing that I was three months pregnant and probably could hang in there only so long. I used to joke that the last person in the show that could be pregnant is Nettie. She has these lines, "I'm nobody's mother." Then I lost the baby November 13th, during previews. I took a few days off and then came back through the opening of the show. A friend asked me, "Why didn't you just check out after that?" But it was healing to be there, to be back at work. I stayed as long as it took them to find somebody else that they were equally as in love with, and they did in Darlesia. But then I did go ahead and leave, because I needed to refocus on my family.

The time I spend offstage—more than an hour in the middle of the show—be challenging in terms of staying connected to the piece. So I listen through the monitors and turn up the monitor volume in my dressing room or go downstairs and listen to the letters between Celie and myself to stay in the scene.

—DARLESIA CEARCY

DARLESIA CEARCY (Nettie): The show premiered December 1st and January 17th was my opening night. My Nettie is the girl and woman who is a visionary. She distinguishes clearly between right and wrong. No matter what the circumstances are surrounding her life or someone else's, she always knows there's something greater on the other side of it. So she is faithful and positive and works toward the better outcome, and she doesn't stay stuck inside the circumstances, or the seeming reality of what's going on. She loves her sister very much, and she's willing to do whatever is necessary to make sure that they have a better life. She's a very intelligent woman, a humanitarian, and has a lot of compassion.

Squeak

GARY GRIFFIN: In this show, Squeak's not played with the tragedy that happens to her in the film and the book. She's a little winner. She may not be the most talented singer in the world, but her spirit is positive and she has a sense of herself that's delightful. And that's why we like her—amongst these women, she's a bright light.

This is my first role ever on the face of the planet. When I got this job, I took an acting class. I said, I don't get on stage and dance without technique. So I want to figure out what I'm doing. A lot of people ask, so what are you going to do now? I feel like, well, I just got here.

—KRISHA MARCANO

KRISHA MARCANO (Squeak): I got the script in the mail, and my agent said, "You have to have a Southern accent. You have to be very country." I thought, I don't even know what that is. I'm from Trinidad.

I read the script for the first time: "You wanna eat da apple offa dis here tree…" I got on the phone and I said, "I'm not going. I am not going. I don't speak like this, I don't know this woman." My agent convinced me to go because I was scared. "It will be good practice," he said.

The first time I read for Gary [Griffin], he said, "Just so you know, you've never met Harpo before. This is the first time you see him, and I want you to read it like you don't know him. I want you to take your voice up seven octaves, I want it to be obnoxious, and you're seventeen years old." I said, "Oh, God." I'm thinking, That information is not what I walked in the room with. I took thirty seconds, and I went extreme. I didn't expect to get the show, so why not? I went extreme and he fell down on the floor.

Squeak has a young spirit, but she's extremely ambitious. She doesn't know much because she's not highly educated, but she doesn't let her high-pitched voice get in her way. If she sees an opportunity to better her situation, she's going to take it, above and beyond love. You can misunderstand that she's dumb and stupid, just by her voice, but in actuality, that's not the case. This is my first acting role ever on the face of the planet. When I got the job, I came back from Atlanta and took an acting class. I don't get on stage as a dancer and dance without technique, so I want to figure out what I'm doing. A lot of people ask me, So what are you going to do now? I feel like, Well, I just got here.

The Church Ladies

Every time I hear Celie sing "I'm beautiful! Yes, I'm beautiful and I'm here," it touches my heart. I grew up hearing that I was ugly, from my friends, from my family, from looking in the mirror. So seeing her come to that strength and self-acceptance is just like arms around me.

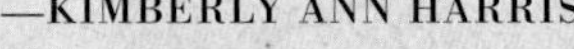

—KIMBERLY ANN HARRIS

As I age through the show, I remind myself of my mother. She always walks really fast and is still having a good time with life. She's always trying to keep up, doesn't want to get left behind. She's got to keep up and see what's going on and stay at the party.

—VIRGINIA ANN WOODRUFF

Alice Walker said that she was channeling for this story and I have taken that on as my personal journey too. To the spirits who are for the highest good of this piece and who bring healing I say yes, and work through me to uphold this gift you have put in our hands, this story of hope and faith and all those wonderful things we should embody to live a great life.

—MAIA NKENGE WILSON

GARY GRIFFIN: To me the Church Ladies are three specific women. We know them from everywhere. But in this community, they are passionate about keeping life in order. They're really an important aspect of our storytelling. So I love the Church Ladies. They're a great device if they reveal humanity. They're a bad device if they're there just to get laughs. Because then it looks like we're making fun of those women, and I never wanted to make fun of them.

I always hate when I see a play and think, Where are the other people? Where are the people who are like the people we know in these towns? These women are those women. They love their religion and their community and their husbands. And they see threats to that. They're also fascinated by Celie. Those women remind you that Celie is a provocative character in this community.

MARSHA NORMAN: When I came into the project, I said to Allee and Stephen and Brenda, "This is the passage-of-time vehicle right here. We're going to use it to tell what's happening, to catch people up in the story and communicate the views of the larger world." I would say things in a clinical, shopping list way, and the three of them would come back with these hilarious, wonderful things for the Ladies to sing. And, of course, those women are so loved by our audience.

KIMBERLY ANN HARRIS (Doris): I think the Church Ladies are Greek chorus slash comic relief slash everywoman—people we know who are busybodies and are very interested in what's going on in the town. There was no television back then, so you had to be amused in some way and this was a good, scandalous way.

MAIA NKENGE WILSON (Jarene): Brenda, Allee, and Stephen, our composers, decided to have us tell the story like a round. One person will start, "I heard about po' chile Celie," and then the other one will say her piece of the story and then the third will say her piece. Then we'll harmonize. It's so clever and so gossipy.

VIRGINIA ANN WOODRUFF (Darlene): As Gary [Griffin] said, we're trying to top each other because our own bit of information is the most important. This is what the scoops, as Kimberly calls them, are all about. We have the scoops. It's like playing the game called Telephone. We all hear it differently. Doris may hear it as something about Celie where Jarene hears something about Mister and I'm hearing something about Celie and Nettie together.

KIMBERLY ANN HARRIS: To me, Virginia's Church Lady, Darlene, likes to laugh. She enjoys herself. I think she would just have the best time if it weren't for the constraints the society at that time put on women. Darlene can be pulled up, but for the most part she loves everybody. She's having a good time. But because the church is such a strong entity in that community, somebody has to be the moral fiber. We've taken that on ourselves.

VIRGINIA ANN WOODRUFF: Maia's Church Lady, Jarene, is somebody who really cares about everyone in the community. So when things happen to individuals, it upsets her. It really bothers her that these bad things have happened. She has a very caring heart.

MAIA NKENGE WILSON: Kimberly's Doris makes me laugh because she's Jarene's best friend. That's how I look at it. Doris has a standard about how things should be, but at the same time she slips, she dips, and dabbles about things. Remember, she's the one who gets a little sip of the moonshine after taking it away from the husbands.

VIRGINIA ANN WOODRUFF: Even in the juke joint, when Sofia goes and dances with Harpo, Doris tries to slip off and dance with Buster. She's doesn't quite make it because the young girl beats her to it, but she wants to dance, too.

MAIA NKENGE WILSON: Doris holds her head high but at the same time she knows. She repeats certain things. What does she say, Kim?

KIMBERLY ANN HARRIS: "Life don't stop just 'cause you leave home."

MAIA NKENGE WILSON: That's what Sofia says. Right when Sofia says it, Doris whispers to us, Don't forget that, don't forget that.

VIRGINIA ANN WOODRUFF: She's saying, We're going to have some fun. That's why we came out today.

Chapter Five

The Libretto

Book by

Marsha Norman

Songs by

Stephen Bray, Brenda Russell, and Allee Willis

BASED UPON THE NOVEL BY ALICE WALKER

Act One · Scene One

Celie and Nettie on their favorite tree

[THE OVERTURE IS HEARD]

BEHIND A SCRIM, IN A TREE, TWO YOUNG SISTERS BEGIN CLAPPING, THEN SING—

CELIE:
Hey, sista, whatcha gon do…

NETTIE:
Goin' down by the river
Gonna play with you

CELIE: *Papa don't like no screamin' round here*

NETTIE:
No lip from da woman when they chug dat beer

NETTIE & CELIE:
Sho nuf sun gon shine *Gonna be*
grown ladies of da marryin' kind
Sho nuf moon gon rise *Like a huckleberry pie* *In da middle of the sky*

Gon be alright *Gon be alright…*

THE SUN COMES UP ON A BRIGHT MORNING. A GOSPEL SOLOIST APPEARS, CALLING THE FAITHFUL TO CHURCH.

SOLOIST: *It's Sunday morning…*

THREE STYLISHLY DRESSED CHURCH LADIES APPEAR AND SING IN RESPONSE.

SOLOIST: *So make a joyful noise*

DARLENE: *Joyful!*

DORIS: *Joyful!*

SOLOIST: *A joyful noise!*
Unto the Lord!

DARLENE: *Lord!*

DORIS: *Lord!*

JARENE: *Lord!*

DARLENE: *Hallelujah!*

SOLOIST: *Today's the day*

SOLOIST & CHURCH LADIES:
God hath made

SOLOIST: *It's Sunday*

DORIS: *Sunday!*

SOLOIST: *It's Sunday*

JARENE: *Sing it, sista!*

DARLENE: *Sunday!*

SOLOIST:
It's Sunday morning! *So make a*

SOLOIST & CHURCH LADIES:
Joyful noise

SOLOIST: *Unto the*

SOLOIST & CHURCH LADIES:
Lord!

THE CONGREGATION BEGINS TO STREAM TOWARD THE CHURCH.

SOLOIST: *When the king threw Daniel in the lion's den*

ENSEMBLE: *The good Lord works*
In mysterious ways!

SOLOIST: *God sent a mighty angel, brought him out again*

ENSEMBLE: *Yes, the good Lord works* *In mysterious ways!*

SOLOIST: *When God saw the wicked he knew what to do*
Said, Noah, bring the animals two by two *I'm gonna keep yo boat afloat for 40 days*

SOLOIST & ENSEMBLE: *Cuz the good Lord works in mysterious ways!*

ENSEMBLE: *Yes, the good Lord works* *In mysterious ways!*

PA: CELIE!

ENSEMBLE: *Ah oom ah ooom*
Ah oom ah ooom *Ah oom ah ooom*
Ah oom ah ooom
Ah oom ah ooom

THE YOUNG GIRLS RUN OFF. THE LAST PEOPLE INTO THE CHURCH ARE NETTIE, AGE 12, AND PA. PA ENTERS AND CALLS TO HIS OTHER DAUGHTER WHO IS NOT YET VISIBLE.

"Make a joyful noise!"

PA: COME ON CELIE, YOU SLOW AS MOLASSES.

NETTIE (LOOKING BACK): CELIE NOT FEELIN' GOOD, PA. SHE GOIN' AS FAST AS SHE CAN.

PA: CELIE!

And finally Celie enters, fourteen years old and hugely pregnant. Pa stomps on to church followed by a handsome man who has his eye on Nettie. The man's children are with him. Nettie goes to help Celie.

CELIE: I'm sorry, Pa.

As Nettie and Celie walk past, the Church Ladies stop Celie. Pa looks back for Nettie.

PA: Nettie!

JARENE: Whatchu gon call your baby, chile?

CELIE: If it's a boy, I'm gon call this one Adam.
An the last one name Olivia.

PA: Celie!

JARENE: Livin' with that man what killed their mother. Now it gon kill them too.

DORIS: *I heard about po'*
Chile Celie — Heard about po'

JARENE: *Already ruint*

DORIS: *Chile Celie*

JARENE: *Two times!*

DORIS: *Heard about po'*

JARENE: *Already ruint*

DORIS: *Chile Celie*

JARENE: *Two times!*

DARLENE:
She only 14 — Years old!

The Church Ladies, now joined by the community, continue chanting, then start singing, music constantly speeding up, turning into a cacophony of gossip by the end.

DORIS: *Who de daddy?*

"Who de daddy?"

JARENE: *Who de daddy?*

DARLENE: *Who de daddy?*

DORIS: *Who de daddy?*

JARENE: *Who de daddy?*

DARLENE: *Who de daddy?*

CHURCH LADIES: *Nobody know!*
I hear her Pa take her chirren
Into the woods and done kilt dem

The Church Ladies join the rest of the congregation in the church.

SOLOIST:
Don't waste your time tryin' to wrassle
with your worldly woe

ENSEMBLE: *The good Lord works*
In mysterious ways!

SOLOIST: *Cause God watchin' over*
you wherever you go

ENSEMBLE:
Yes, the good Lord works
In mysterious ways!

SOLOIST: *If your po' back breakin'*

ENSEMBLE: *Ooooh*

SOLOIST: *Under all that weight*

ENSEMBLE: *Oooh*

SOLOIST: *St. Peter gonna lift it*

ENSEMBLE: *Oooh*

SOLOIST: *At the pearly gate*

ENSEMBLE: *Ooooh*

SOLOIST: *Let the spirit walk beside*
you on your darkest days

ENSEMBLE: *Oh, the good Lord*
Works in mysterious ways!

PREACHER: Now none of us know what the Lord's got planned for us, no sir. So I want y'all to quit your moanin' and your groanin'. Just throw away your handkerchiefs. Put your hand in His and follow where He leads. Have mercy! That's what I'm talkin' about! Don't you worry now. Cause no matter what happen the good Lord is walkin' witcha.

ENSEMBLE: *Walkin'!*

The congregation raises their voices to God

PREACHER: And He talkin' witcha too.

ENSEMBLE: *Talkin'!*

CHURCH LADIES: *Walkin' witcha ~ Talkin' witcha When the devil start squawkin' witcha ~ God won't quitcha ~ No he won't!*

ENSEMBLE: *Yes He works!*

SOLOIST: *Whoa He walkin'*

ENSEMBLE: *Yes He works!*

SOLOIST: *Yes He walk*

ENSEMBLE: *Yes He works!*

SOLOIST: *Every day*

ENSEMBLE: *Yes He works!*

SOLOIST: *Oh in every way*

Soloist continues wailing throughout the following to the end of the song.

ENSEMBLE: *Yes He works!*

CHURCH LADIES: *Walkin' witcha*

ENSEMBLE: *Yes He works!*

CHURCH LADIES: *Talkin' witcha*

ENSEMBLE: *Yes He works!*

CHURCH LADIES: *When the devil start ~ Squawkin' witcha*

ENSEMBLE: *Yes He works!*

CHURCH LADIES: *God won't quitcha ~ No He won't*

ENSEMBLE: *Yes He works!*

CHURCH LADIES: *Works!*

ENSEMBLE: *Yes He works!*

CHURCH LADIES: *Works!*

ENSEMBLE: *Yes He works!*

ENSEMBLE: *Works!*

CHURCH LADIES: *Walkin' witcha*

ENSEMBLE: *Yes He works!*

ENSEMBLE: *Works!*

CHURCH LADIES: *Talkin' witcha*

ENSEMBLE: *Yes He works!*

ENSEMBLE: *Works!*

CHURCH LADIES: *When the devil start ~ Squawkin' witcha*

ENSEMBLE: *Yes He works!*

ENSEMBLE: *Works!*

CHURCH LADIES: *God won't quitcha ~ No He won't!*

ENSEMBLE: *Yes He works!*

ENSEMBLE: *Works!*

SOLOIST: *Yes He*

ENSEMBLE: *Yes He works!*

ENSEMBLE: *Work!*

SOLOIST: *Work!*

Suddenly, Celie cries out in pain in response to a contraction.

CELIE: Dear God!

ENSEMBLE: *Works!*

Celie looks around for help, grabs Nettie's hand and screams again.

CELIE: Dear God!

SOLOIST: *You know God works...*

Celie indicates to Nettie that they don't have any time to lose. The baby is coming. They move toward the door and they leave as everyone sings, claps, and shouts louder. Pa grabs his hat and leaves the church.

ENSEMBLE: *In mysterious ways—*

DARLENE: *So make a*

ENSEMBLE: *Joy*

DARLENE: *Joyful*

DORIS: *Noise*

JARENE: *Joyful noise ~ Throw your hands up*

DARLENE: *I said a ~ Joyful ~ Noise*

JARENE: *Get up on your feet*

DORIS: *Joyful noise ~ Joyful*

JARENE: *Joyful*

DORIS: *Joyful*

JARENE: *Joyful*

PREACHER: *Come on! Come on church!*

ENSEMBLE: *Unto the Lord ~ Unto the ~ Lord!*

Applause.

ENSEMBLE: *Ah oom ah ooom ~ Ah oom ah ooom ~ Ah oom ah ooom*

WE HEAR A BABY CRY. A SHED APPEARS. CELIE AND NETTIE SIT ON A BALE OF HAY, CELIE HOLDING THE BABY SHE HAS JUST GIVEN BIRTH TO.

CELIE: *Got nuthin' to give you*
but a prayer ◦ *God's gonna see you*
through ◦ *To part with you more*
than I can bear ◦ *But somebody*
gonna love you

Sweet baby sweet ◦ *This much I know*
is true ◦ *Sleep baby sleep* ◦ *Cause*
somebody gonna love you

Yes, I'm always gonna love you

PA ENTERS THE SHED.

PA: YOU DONE IN HERE?

CELIE: I HAD A BOY BABY, PA. HIS NAME ADAM.

PA: WELL GIVE HIM TO ME, THEN. I'LL GET RID OF IT SAME AS THE FIRST ONE.

CELIE: PLEASE, PA.

PA: YOU CAN'T TAKE CARE NO BABY. NOW YOUR MAMA'S DEAD, YOU GOT ALL HER WORK TO DO PLUS YOUR OWN.

NETTIE:
I'LL HELP CELIE, PA.

NETTIE TRIES TO INTERVENE, BUT PA JERKS HER AWAY IN A ROUGH WAY.

PA:
YOU GIMME THAT BABY!

CELIE RESPONDS QUICKLY TO PROTECT NETTIE.

CELIE:
DON'T HURT NETTIE, PA.

PA GRABS THE BABY, AND LEAVES THE GIRLS ALONE. NETTIE HELPS CELIE PUT HER DRESS ON.

CELIE:
YOU THINK PA KILL MY BABIES?

Celie clutches her baby, Adam

NETTIE:
NO, CELIE. HE GIVE 'EM AWAY.

CELIE:
HOW YOU KNOW THAT?

NETTIE:
IT'S NOT SOMETHIN' I KNOW. IT'S SOMETHIN' I BELIEVE. YOU WANT ME TO STAY HERE WITH YOU?

CELIE:
NO. YOU GO ON. I JUST BE A MINUTE.

NETTIE LEAVES.
THE SHED REVOLVES AWAY AND THE SOLOIST APPEARS AGAIN, OR IS PERHAPS OFFSTAGE, THIS TIME SINGING IN A MORE DISTANT, THOUGHTFUL WAY, AS IF SHE IS A MEMORY. THE ENSEMBLE MAY SING FROM THE WINGS.

SOLOIST: *You know that Shadrach,*
Meshack, and Abednego...

CELIE LOOKS UP TO GOD.

CELIE: DEAR GOD. I AM ONLY—I AM FOURTEEN YEARS OLD.

ENSEMBLE: *The good Lord works*
◦ *In mysterious ways!*

CELIE: I AM—

SOLOIST: *Walked out of the fire* ◦
With their faith aglow

CELIE (OVER THE ENSEMBLE):
I HAVE ALWAYS BEEN A GOOD GIRL.

ENSEMBLE: *Yes, the good Lord*
works ◦ *In mysterious ways!*

CELIE: MAYBE YOU CAN GIVE ME A SIGN LETTING ME KNOW WHAT IS HAPPENING TO ME.

CELIE LEAVES THE STAGE.

SOLOIST: *L'il David was a*
shepherd ◦ *Who was pure and brave* ◦
With sling and stone he sent ◦
Goliath to his grave

SOLOIST: *His only suit of armor*
was a song of praise

ENSEMBLE: *Yes, the good Lord*
works ◦ *In mysterious ways!*

Scene Two · The Marriage

The girls dream of what the future may bring

Pa's store appears.
Celie and Nettie appear.

NETTIE & CELIE: *Hey sista, whatcha gon do ~ Goin down by the river ~ Gonna play with you*

A group of boys appears.

CELIE: Which one them boys you want? You so grown up and pretty now, it's time for you to get married, have one good year before you get big.

They see Mister talking to Pa.

NETTIE: I can't get married, I'm still in school. Who that man talking to Pa?

CELIE: Girl at church say he lookin' for a new wife take care his mean chirren.

NETTIE: Well I see where they get that mean from. Look at Him holdin' his whip like he got a horse waiting somewhere. You see any horse?

CELIE (laughs, then): You don't want to get married?

The Pa and Mister conversation is over. Mister exits.

NETTIE: *I wanna know how the world goes ~ How far is the moon? ~ How the sky changes color? ~ Hope I find out soon*

NETTIE: What you want?

CELIE: *Wanna sit and do nothing ~ Make you a new dress ~ Hope my babies are happy ~ Some place God will bless*

PA: Celie! Get to work!

Pa goes into the store.

NETTIE: *Ain't no need to discuss*

CELIE: *It ain't worth a big fuss*

NETTIE & CELIE: *Whatever come to us ~ Is in God's hands ~ When I lay me down to sleep ~ I will say my prayer ~ That God love me so deep ~ He will promise our souls to keep ~ Together ~ I say a prayer*

Another day. Mister enters the store to talk to Pa.

PA: Why you want to know so much about tobacco?

MISTER: Thinkin' about plantin' it.

PA: You is not. Now what you doin' here?

Pa and Mister look at the girls.

MISTER: *I want to marry Nettie ~ She a sweet young girl*

PA: She too young.

MISTER: *She the cutest thing in this ~ Whole world*

PA: She gonna be a teacher. You can have Celie though. She too old to be livin' at home.

CELIE: *Maybe I'll have a garden ~ Where birds come to sing*

MISTER: I don't want Celie. She ugly.

Mister leaves the store.

CELIE: *Know a finch from a sparrow ~ Fix a broken wing*

NETTIE: *I wanna hear your birds sing*

CELIE: *Wanna hear your school bell ring*

NETTIE & CELIE: *No matter what life bring ~ Us in God's hands*

Another day. Mister returns to talk to Pa. The Church Ladies are in the store.

PA: Whyn't you quit comin' round here and just go marry your Shug Avery?

The Church Ladies leave the store.

CHURCH LADIES: *Shug Avery!*

NETTIE: Who Shug Avery?

CHURCH LADIES: *Shug Avery!*

CELIE: She Mister ol' girlfriend.

MISTER: Shug Avery not a child-raisin' woman, you know that. She the Queen Honeybee.

PA: She a low-down whore is what everybody say. You lookin' for a new Shug Avery, you better go to Memphis. All we got here is one pretty girl you can't never have, and one ugly girl . . .

PA (at the same time as Mister): Can work like a man.

MISTER: *I-I-I-I ~ I-I-I-I really want that girl*

PA: I told you no!

Pa exits.
Mister watches Nettie.

Pa gives Celie to Mister

NETTIE & CELIE
(AT THE SAME TIME AS MISTER):
When I ~ Lay me down to ~ Sleep ~ I will ~ Say my prayer ~ That God love ~ Me ~ So deep ~ He will ~ Promise ~ Our souls ~ To keep together ~ I'll say a prayer

MISTER: *I wanna ~ Marry ~ Nettie ~ She a ~ Sweet young girl ~ She the ~ Sweetest thing ~ In this ~ Whole ~ Wide world ~ I-I-I-I ~ I really want that girl*

MISTER EXITS.

CELIE: YOU WANT ANY KIDS?

NETTIE: SOMEDAY I GUESS. I KNOW YOU DO.

CELIE: DOCTOR SAY I CAN'T HAVE NO MORE KIDS. SO I THINK GOD JUST WANT ME TO TAKE CARE THINGS.

THEY CLIMB THE TREE.

NETTIE: *We'll live in big houses*

CELIE: *Put swings in the trees*

NETTIE: *Braid up your gray hair*

NETTIE & CELIE: *In the cool of the breeze ~ And one day ~ Our children will sing—*

NETTIE & CELIE: *When I lay me down to sleep ~ I will say my prayer ~ That God love me so deep ~ He will promise our souls to keep ~ Together ~ I say a prayer ~ I'll say our prayer*

MISTER AND PA ENTER.

PA: CELIE! COME ON DOWN HERE. MISTER WANT TO LOOK AT YOU.

MISTER: NO I DON'T NEITHER.

PA: YOU THINK YOU GON GIT SOME FRESH GIRL TO MARRY YOU NOW? CELIE!

NETTIE (GRABS HER): NO, CELIE!

CELIE: IF I DON'T GO WITH HIM, HE'LL TAKE YOU AND YOU'LL NEVER FINISH SCHOOL.

MISTER GETS HIS FIRST LOOK AT CELIE.

MISTER: SHE WORSE THAN I THOUGHT. SHE DON'T EVEN LOOK LIKE KIN TO NETTIE. MAYBE I—

PA: MAYBE YOU PUT CELIE IN CHARGE OF YOUR CHIRREN FORE THEY GIT BIG ENOUGH TO KILL YOU IN THE NIGHT.

MISTER: NAW, I THINK I JUST BUY THAT COW YOU GOT DOWN BY THE CRIB.

PA: YOU TAKE CELIE, I'LL GIVE YOU THAT COW.

MISTER LOOKS AT BOTH THE WOMEN.

MISTER: COME ON, GIRL.

NETTIE RUNS TO EMBRACE CELIE.

NETTIE:
I'LL COME SEE YOU EVERY—

BUT JUST AS THEY REACH EACH OTHER, MISTER PULLS CELIE AWAY AND WHIPS HER WITH THE RIDING CROP.

MISTER: I SAID COME ON!

MISTER WALKS OFF WITH CELIE.

NETTIE: HE CAN'T HIT HER!

PA: SHE GON BE HIS WIFE. HE DO WHAT HE WANT.

PA TAKES NETTIE INTO THE STORE. THE CHURCH LADIES ENTER. THEY HAVE NOT SEEN THE WHIPPING.

JARENE: *And what about ~ That fine Mister? ~ What about that ~ Fine Mister?*

DORIS: *Marryin' that po' ~ Homely child ~ Uh!*

JARENE: *What about ~ That fine Mister?*

DORIS: *Marryin' ~ That po' ~ Homely child ~ Uh*

DARLENE: *She gonna work ~ Like ~ A mule*

JARENE: *What about ~ That fine Mister?*

DORIS: *Marryin' ~ That po' ~ Homely child ~ Uh*

JARENE: *He got ~ Two cows ~ Out that deal!*

JARENE: *Have mercy!*

DORIS: *Have mercy!*

DARLENE: *Have mercy!*

JARENE: *Have mercy!*

DORIS: *Have mercy!*

DARLENE: *Have mercy!*

JARENE: *Say what gon come ~ O' that sweet Nettie*

DORIS: *'Lone with that ~ Lech of a man ~ Hmmph!*

DARLENE: *They two ~ Unfortunate gals*

CHURCH LADIES: *They need a chariot today ~ To swing low and carry them away!*

Scene Three · Mister's House

"Sweep this barn, milk that cow, water from the well, fields to plow..."

CELIE FOLLOWS MISTER TOWARD HIS HOUSE FROM THE LAST SCENE. WE SEE FIELD HANDS AT WORK.

MISTER: THERE'S MY FIELD, THERE'S MY CATTLE AND THERE'S MY MEN.

FIELD HANDS: *He want his hamhocks hot — And his lemonade cold — Don't want to hear no lip — Just do what you're told — Pluck them chickens — Scrub them pots and pans — You gonna churn that butter — Til it cramp your hands — If you think hard work — Been doggin' you before — Get ready for the big dog!*

MISTER: THIS MY HOUSE.

MISTER: *Fix that*

FIELD HANDS: *Work!*

MISTER: *Broken window 'fore the*

FIELD HANDS: *Work!*

MISTER:
Rain come in — You got to

FIELD HANDS: *Work!*

MISTER:
Kill that rat — With this here...

FIELD HANDS: *Work!*

MISTER: *Rollin' pin*

MISTER: *Mop this floor*

FIELD HANDS: *Humm!*

MISTER: *Pick up — All this mess*
You know that

FIELD HANDS: *Humm!*

MISTER & FIELD HANDS:
Cleanliness

MISTER: *Next to*

MISTER & FIELD HANDS:
Godliness

FIELD HANDS: *If you think hard work been doggin' you before — Get ready for the big dog! — Hunh!*

HARPO THROWS A ROCK AT CELIE.

CELIE: OWW!

MISTER: *Sweep this barn*

CELIE: *Nettie go*

MISTER: *Milk that cow*

CELIE: *To the schoolhouse*

MISTER: *Water from the well*

CELIE: *Get her*

MISTER: *Fields to plow*

CELIE: *College degree*

MISTER: *Brush my horse*

CELIE: *Nettie teachin'*

MISTER: *Feed that pig*

CELIE: *The children*

MISTER: *Tree to chop*

CELIE: *To spell*

MISTER: *Ditch to dig*

CELIE: *Tennessee*

MISTER: *Fetch them eggs*

CELIE: *Won't be time*

MISTER: *Pitch that hay*

CELIE: *For a garden*

MISTER: *Patch the fence*
so the Billy

CELIE: *No birds*

MISTER: *Don't stray*

CELIE: *Gonna sing*

MISTER: *Pull the turnips*

CELIE: *Won't be time*

MISTER: *Hose the greens*

CELIE: *For my readin'*

MISTER: *Feed the baby goats*

CELIE: *Til the last one weans*

FIELD HANDS:
Get ready for the big dog!

MISTER: *Work!*

FIELD HANDS: *Hunh!*

THE KIDS RUN PAST THEM. EACH ONE LOOKING WORSE THAN THE NEXT. MISTER YELLS AT THEM THROUGHOUT CELIE'S SINGING.

MISTER: HARPO! I WARNED YOU ABOUT THIS. I GON BEAT YOU CLEAN TO DEATH. GET MY BELT!

HARPO: NO! PA!

CELIE: *When I lay me down to sleep*
I will say my prayer

MISTER: YOU THROW YOUR FOOD ON THE FLOOR, YOU GON EAT IT OFF THE FLOOR, YOU LITTLE PIG.

CELIE: *That God love me so deep*
He will promise our souls to keep

GIRL: DADDY, CAN I HAVE

MISTER: YOU GET NUTHIN' FROM ME, GIRL. AND THE NEXT ONE OF YOU SAYS A WORD GETS TIED TO THE FENCE POST.

CELIE: *Together*

MISTER: *Bedroom's upstairs*

CELIE: *I say a prayer*

MISTER DRAGS HER TO THE BEDROOM.

FIELD HANDS: *He like his bath real hot Like it bout to boil You got to rub his feet With some liniment oil Shave his whiskers Hope it's understood That you best not cut him Or he beat you good If you think hard work been doggin' you before Get ready for the big dog!*

MISTER PUSHES CELIE DOWN ONTO THE BED.

ANOTHER DAY. CELIE ENTERS. YOUNG HARPO ENTERS.

CELIE: HARPO, WOULD YOU GET ME SOME WATER, PLEASE.

HARPO: YES, M'AM.

HARPO EXITS. CELIE TAKES CLOTHES OFF A CLOTHESLINE. NETTIE RUNS ONSTAGE.

NETTIE: CELIE!!!!!!!!

NETTIE RUNS TO CELIE.

CELIE: NETTIE! I MISSED YOU SO MUCH.

NETTIE: CELIE, I CAN'T LIVE WITH PA NO MORE. HE'S ALWAYS AFTER ME. YOU THINK MISTER LET ME LIVE HERE WITH YOU?

CELIE: I DON'T KNOW.

MISTER APPEARS.

MISTER: WHAT GOIN' ON HERE?

CELIE: NETTIE NEED A PLACE TO STAY.

MISTER: WELL NOW. I ALWAYS HAD ROOM FOR NETTIE. (PUTTING ON HIS HAT) MAYBE SHE CAN MAKE MY KIDS MIND. (THEN TO CELIE) AND WHEN YOU GON SEW SOME NEW CLOTHES FOR THESE CHIRREN? I SHAMED TO BE SEEN WITH THEM. GO INTO TOWN AND BUY SOME CLOTH.

HE LEAVES.

NETTIE: I DON'T LIKE HOW MISTER TREAT YOU. IT LIKE YOU BURIED IN THAT HOUSE.

CELIE: IF I REALLY BURIED IT BE BETTER. I NOT HAVE TO WORK. BUT I FINISH MOST NIGHTS BY TEN. THEN WHILE HE ON TOP OF ME, I LAY THERE, THINK BOUT YOU. WONDER IF YOU SAFE.

NETTIE: WELL, I WISH I COULD STAY AND HELP YOU, BUT I GOT TO GET TO SCHOOL.

CELIE: IT'S OK. YOU GO.

NETTIE GETS HER SCHOOL BOOKS.

NETTIE: BUT WHEN I GET BACK, I'M GONNA READ YOU A STORY, WHILE YOU SIT IN A CHAIR.

CELIE: I GOT PIES TO MAKE BUT I LIKE TO BE READ TO.

THEY HUG AND NETTIE GOES OFF. BUT MISTER HAS NOT GONE AWAY. HE WAITS FOR NETTIE AND THEN APPEARS.

MISTER: *You got some pretty teeth, Nettie*

SHE IS SURPRISED BUT TRIES NOT TO LET ON. EYES TO THE GROUND

NETTIE: CELIE HAS PRETTY TEETH TOO, DON'T YOU THINK?

MISTER: *And your skin dazzle my eyes Like the moon light the night*

NETTIE (STILL REFUSING TO LOOK AT HIM): THANK YOU.

MISTER: *That's a real pretty dress, Nettie*

NETTIE: YOU MARRIED TO MY SISTER.

MISTER: *And them shoes look just right On dem pretty little feets*

NETTIE: I GOT TO GET TO SCHOOL.

MISTER: *Need some sugar for my sweet tooth, Nettie*

NETTIE: DON'T COME OVER HERE.

MISTER: *When you gonna let me lick your lollipop?*

HE ADVANCES IN ON HER.

NETTIE: PLEASE! NO! LEAVE ME ALONE! CELIE!

NETTIE ESCAPES HIS GRASP AND RUNS, DROPPING HER SCHOOL BOOKS.

MISTER (LAUGHS): DON'T FORGET YOUR BOOKS, GIRL!

MISTER GOES AFTER NETTIE. CELIE ENTERS LOOKING FOR NETTIE.

CELIE: NETTIE?!

CELIE RUNS OFF LOOKING FOR NETTIE. NETTIE RUNS ON, THINKING SHE HAS ESCAPED MISTER. MISTER APPEARS BEHIND HER. THEY STRUGGLE. SHE KICKS HIM. HE GROANS AND FALLS TO THE GROUND.

NETTIE: Celie!

Nettie runs off. Celie runs on and sees Mister on the ground. She runs after Nettie. Mister, doubled up in pain, runs and follows them. Celie runs on looking for Nettie. Nettie runs on and into Celie's arms.

NETTIE: Celie!

The girls embrace. Mister enters.

MISTER: She got to go!

Mister grabs them. The girls hang onto each other.

CELIE: No!

NETTIE: Celie! No!

CELIE: *Dear God*

Mister separates them, pushing Nettie to the ground. Mister starts toward Nettie.

CELIE: *Don't take my Nettie!*

Celie grabs Mister. Mister raises his hand to hit Celie.

MISTER: You ain't never gonna hear from her.

Nettie jumps up to stop him. Mister and Nettie struggle.

CELIE: *Don't do this*

Mister gets a hold of Nettie and begins to push her out.

CELIE: Don't hurt her!

MISTER: You even try to find her, and she be the one to pay.

NETTIE: Don't forget me, Celie.

Mister throws Nettie out.

"What kind of God are you?"

CELIE: Nettie, write me!

Mister throws rocks at Nettie.

NETTIE: I'll write you every day. Nothin' but death will keep me from it.

CELIE: Nettie!

Nettie runs away. Mister starts toward the house.

MISTER:
You sister dead to you. Dead!

CELIE (to Mister):
You can't do this! You can't do this!

Celie grabs Mister. He hits her. Celie falls to the ground. Mister leaves her and continues to walk back to the house. Underscore continues as Celie is paralyzed by the truth of what has just happened. Nettie is gone. She sinks to the ground. She bows her head. Then looks up.

CELIE: *Dear God What you done with my sister? How this play in your plan? Won't you bring back my Nettie? You the only one who can*

Why you take my heart fom me? Make me live this wretched life? Now you got to tell me why you put me here dear God

I never ask for anything But I'm asking for this If I'm really a lily of the field You will answer my prayers Or you're no God at all!

Music and lights change to indicate time passing. A mailbox appears. It is 5 years later. Celie stands beside the mailbox. She opens the mailbox door, but Mister appears from nowhere and shuts it hard.

MISTER: What you think you doin'? You touch that mailbox and I'll kill you, girl.

The mailbox disappears.

CELIE: *So many winters gray and summers blue*

She must be dead.

What kind of God are you?

Celie turns. Harpo appears.

Scene Four · Sofia

"A pretty name, Sofia, So-fi-a..."

It's 1919. Celie, now 22, speaks to Harpo as he watches someone coming up to the gate. Harpo is 17.

CELIE: Harpo, I ain't never seen you so bright.

HARPO: See that girl comin'? I'm gon marry that girl.

CELIE: She good and strong, I can see that. Earth shake.

Sofia enters.

HARPO: Miss Celie, this here Sofia.

SOFIA: Nice to meet you, m'am.

CELIE: You too.

Mister enters with buddies, ignoring Harpo and Sofia.

HARPO: *Pa. This here is Sofia. A pretty name, Sofia, So-fi-a.*

MISTER (to Sofia): Look like you done got yourself in trouble.

SOFIA: No, suh, I ain't in no trouble. Big though... Big though.

MISTER: And who the daddy?

SOFIA: Harpo!

MISTER: How he know that?

SOFIA: *He know cuz he the only one.*

HARPO: *Sofia, So–fi–a*

MISTER: Celie, get me some lemonade.

Sofia watches in amazement as Celie timidly goes for lemonade. Celie hands Mister a glass of lemonade. He waves it away.

MISTER: Ain't cold enough.

Celie tries to hide the shame she feels as Sofia watches her carry the glass out again.

MISTER: You want my Harpo cause your daddy done put you out. You bout to live in the street!

SOFIA: I ain't livin' in no street. I take my baby to my sister and her husband's. I don't stay nowhere they don't treat me right.

She heads toward the steps, looking back.

SOFIA: Come on, Harpo!

MISTER (to Harpo): Don't you move, boy.

Harpo feels caught in between them and is afraid to move. But it's clear he isn't going. Sofia is covering her hurt. She doesn't want to leave without Harpo. Everyone is stuck in place, til finally—

CELIE (to Sofia): Would you like some lemonade?

Sofia is grateful to have an ally. She takes a sip of the lemonade.

SOFIA: At least somebody around here knows how to treat a lady!

She waits a moment then turns on her heel.

SOFIA: Don't make me wait too long, Harpo!

She exits, handing him the glass. He starts to follow.

MISTER: Harpo!

Mister looks at Harpo a moment, then stands up and storms into the house, disgusted. Harpo and Celie stand there a minute together, then Harpo leaves to follow Sofia. Celie smiles suddenly. She has never seen anything like this before.

CELIE: *Dear God ∞ I love this woman! ∞ My friend Sofia ∞ Harpo he loves her ∞ And he smile anytime he see her ∞ Ain't never seen such a vision! ∞ Cow bossin' the bull around ∞ Ain't afraid a nothin' ∞ When she lay her law down ∞ Took Harpo's hand ∞ Now she havin' his babies ∞ She rule the house an it drivin' him crazy ∞ She give him lip and now he just fit to be tied*

On another day—in the field—three years later.

Mister and field hands enter. Harpo is working silently, but furiously, taking out some big kind of anger on the field.

MISTER: You got some kinda war goin' on down at your house, boy? I could hear Sofia yellin' at you all morning. What'd you say?

Mister

Harpo

HARPO: It don't matter what I say. She do what she want.

MISTER: Women in Sofia family all crazy, you know that.

Mister and field hands exit. Celie has been listening in.

HARPO: What you think, Miss Celie?

CELIE: I think you happy with Sofia, you been married three years and you still whistle and sing.

HARPO: I want her to jump when I call her, like you do when Pa call you.

CELIE (hangs her head): Well, if that's what you want, then you gon have to beat her.

HARPO: Beat her.

The Church Ladies appear. There is incredible noise from Sofia's and Harpo's.

DORIS: *I heard about Sofia and Harpo*

JARENE: *Sound like a twister set down*

DARLENE: *He say he kicked by a mule*

CHURCH LADIES: *He run into a tree and her name Sofia*

At Sofia's house Celie approaches carefully, the house has sustained some big damage. Sofia sees Celie.

SOFIA: You told Harpo to beat me?

CELIE: I'm sorry.

SOFIA: I love Harpo, God knows I do. But I'll kill him dead before I let him or anybody beat me.

SOFIA: *All my life I had to fight ~ I had to fight my daddy ~ I had to fight my brothers, my cousins, my uncles too ~ But I never, never, never thought I had to fight in my own house!*

I feel sorry for you ~ To tell you the truth ~ You remind me of my mama ~ Under your husband's thumb ~ Naw, you under your husband's foot ~ And what he say go ~ Why you so scared ~ I'll never know

If a man ~ Raise his hand ~ Hell no! Hell no!

Girl child ain't safe ~ In a family o' mens ~ Sick'n tired how a woman ~ Still live like a slave ~ Lawd ~ Ahh, you better learn how to fight back ~ While you still alive ~ You show them girl ~ And beat back that jive

Cause when a man ~ Just don't give a damn ~ Hell no! ~ Hell no!

CELIE: What you gonna do now?

SOFIA: My sisters gon come get me. I think I need me a vacation up on out of here.

CELIE: But Harpo's your husband. You got to stay with him. I know you love him.

SOFIA: *When that man used to touch me ~ He clam on top and start to rock me away ~ Lord knows I still loves him ~ But he try to make me mind ~ And I just ain't that kind ~ Hell no!*

CELIE: Sometimes my husband get on me so hard it hurt me all over, but he my husband so I just talk to my old maker. This life'll soon be over. Heaven lasts always.

SOFIA: What you ought to do is bash Mister's head open. Think on heaven later. You cain't stay here, girl. Sistas!

Sofia's sisters appear.

SISTER 1: *Hell no!*

SISTER 2: *Hell no!*

SISTER 3: *Hell no!*

SISTER 4:*Hell no!*

SISTER 5: *Hell no!*

SISTER 1: *Hell no!*

SISTER 6: *Hell no!*

ALL SISTERS: *Hell no! ~ Let's go! ~ Hell no! ~ Let's go!*

SISTER 6: *Gonna be your rock ~ Gonna be your tree*

SISTER 4: *Somethin' to hold on to ~ In your time of need*

SISTER 6: *Girl, you too good ~ For that man!*

ALL SISTERS: *Damn that man*

SISTER 2: *Gonna take you away*

ALL SISTERS: *Take my hand ~ Sista, you got to go*

SISTER 5: *Don't be no fool ~ Don't waste no time*

SISTER 1: *Any man who hurts you ~ Ain't worth a dime*

SISTER 2: *Well he won't know ~ Til you gone*

ALL SISTERS: *She be gone*

SISTER 5: *What he throwin' away*

ALL SISTERS: *He be wrong ~ Sista, you got to go!*

The sisters sing to Celie.

SOFIA: *Girl, you too good ~ For that man ~ Let me take you away*

ALL SISTERS: *Sistas*

SOFIA: *Let me take you away ~ Sistas Ah, take you away*

ALL SISTERS: *Sistas*

SOFIA: *Let me take you away*

ALL SISTERS: *Sistas*

SISTER 4: *Hey!*

ALL SISTERS: *Sista, you got to say...*

SISTERS & SOFIA: *...Hellllll...*

SOFIA: *Hellllll...*

SISTERS & SOFIA: *No!*

Celie watches Sofia, her sisters and children roll out of sight toward the road.

CELIE: Dear God...

Outside. Sofia's march music returns as Mister appears with his field hands, talking to Harpo, who has a beat-up face.

MISTER
(looking at the bruised Harpo):
What happened to you?

HARPO: Mule kicked me.

MISTER
(shakes his head and chuckles):
Again?

Mister and field hands exit. Celie can't believe what has happened.

CELIE (to Harpo): You gon let Sofia go?

HARPO: I have to. I can't stop her.

CELIE: What you gon do then?

HARPO: I'm gon tear down this house she made me build, and make myself a juke joint.

Harpo's buddies enter.

CELIE: Out here in the woods?

HARPO: Juke joint supposed to be in the woods.

CELIE: Nobody come.

"Sista, you got to say, Hellllll no!"

Scene Five · Betty Brown

Squeak shows up at Harpo's Juke Joint

At the Juke joint—1922—Celie is 27, Mister is 37. Harpo 22. Harpo's buddies heave hammers and saws as they rebuild Harpo's house into a juke joint. But Harpo is just sitting there.

BUDDY 1: Harpo, you sleep?

BUDDY 2: He dreamin' up more work for us to do.

BUDDY 3: You ask folk to help you build somethin', you sposed to work too.

BUDDY 4: You sick?

HARPO: Nah. I ain't sick.
Brown-legged woman put a spell on me

BUDDY & OTHER BUDDY:
Oh, Brown Betty!

BUDDY 3: Time you forgit about Sofia.

BUDDY 4: She's not comin' back.

HARPO: *She chop me down like an ol' oak tree*

HARPO & BUDDIES: *Don't matter if she ∼ Big-legged, brown-eyed ∼ Big-eyed, brown-legged ∼ Whatever she done, that girl sho was fine*

The two buddies exit with the house door. New day. A cute young woman comes up, her eyes on all these men.

SQUEAK: What y'all buildin' here?

HARPO: Juke joint.

SQUEAK: Ya'll need a waitress?

HARPO: Sho do. Be done a week from today. You come back then.

SQUEAK: All right then, I will. I got my outfit already. You like yella? My name's Squeak.

Squeak leaves.

HARPO: *Gonna make you holler like a wildcat do*

HARPO & BUDDIES:
Oh, Brown Betty!

HARPO: *When I throw my mojo down on you*

HARPO & BUDDIES: *Don't matter if she ∼ Big-legged, brown-eyed ∼ Big-eyed, brown-legged... ∼ Whatever she is, that girl sho is fine*

BUDDIES: *Whatever she is, that girl sho is fine ∼ Huh!*

New day. Mister appears, with the mail.

MISTER: How y'all comin' down here?

HARPO: Not bad.

Mister keeps going, his eyes on one of his letters.

MISTER: Shug?

Quickly, he opens the letter and reads through it.

MISTER: Shug Avery comin'. (now calling) Celie! Celie!

Mister walks off. Squeak sits with Harpo as he works.

SQUEAK: Who gon sing at your juke joint?

HARPO: Whoever want to, I guess.

SQUEAK: I always wanted to sing.

HARPO: What you sing about, bein' skinny?

SQUEAK: You git Shug Avery come sing here you make a lot of money. She comin' to town, you know. Everybody getting ready to lock up they men, my mama say.

HARPO: Uh-huh.

SQUEAK: Is it true her daddy the preacher? Only he don't speak to her no more on account of having all them babies and not marryin' they daddy? Who they daddy, you know?

HARPO: He my daddy, I think. Only *his* daddy wouldn't let him marry her.

SQUEAK: Then Shug Avery practically your mama. She sing for you, Harpo. I know she will. You so pretty.

Men laugh.

HARPO: Men ain't pretty.

SQUEAK: You is.

There is an awkward moment. Suddenly, she starts to sing. The men are her backup band.

SQUEAK: *If you wanna eat the apple offa dis here tree...*

HARPO & BUDDIES: *Yeah, Brown Betty!*

SQUEAK: *...don't bring nothing but your sweet stuff home to me.*

Squeak begins her dance.

HARPO & BUDDIES:
Don't matter if she big-legged... ∼ Big-legged ∼ Brown-eyed ∼ Brown-eyed ∼ Big-eyed ∼ Big-eyed ∼ Brown-legged ∼ Brown-legged...

HARPO:
Whatever she is, that girl sho is fine

Scene Six: Shug Avery

In Mister's bedroom. Mister is getting ready as fast as he can. He sings toward Celie, who is elsewhere in the house.

MISTER: *Where my shirt? ❧ Where my hat? ❧ Where you put my braces at? ❧ Fix my tie ❧ Press my pants ❧ Ugly man ain't got no chance!*

CELIE: *What is you fussin' for, Mister? ❧ What you care about 'sides yourself?*

MISTER: *Celie head full o' rocks ❧ There's holes in my Sunday socks*

The Church Ladies enter.

MISTER: *Shug Avery comin' to town!*

JARENE: *Shug Avery comin' to town!*

But on the street in town, not everybody's as happy as he is.

CHURCH LADIES: *Lock up all your mens ❧ And your young boys too ❧ Shug ain't got no friends ❧ 'Cept the ones she screw*

CHURCH LADIES & MISTER: *Shug Avery comin' to town!*

CHURCH LADIES: *Shug comin'!*

MISTER: Mmmm, gonna get me

CHURCH LADIES: *Shug comin'!*

MISTER: Some sugar today!

Celie enters with his pants, shirt, and tie.

CELIE: *Sharp as a tack ❧ With your hair slicked back ❧ Spit on your shoes ❧ What you tryin' to do?*

The Church Ladies see Mister now, all proud. They just know he's going after Shug. The men see it, too, only they wish it was them going after her.

CHURCH LADIES: *That Mister sho do shine ❧ When Shug come cross that county line*

MAN: *Ain't no other woman like Shug*

MAN: *Like Shug*

MEN: *Oh, Lord let me cross ❧ Into her promised land*

The ladies follow Mister. Disapproving and disgusted. The men follow, too. It's two worlds here, the women and the men.

CHURCH LADIES: *Drinkin' the gin ❧ Lovin' all the mens ❧ Strumpet in a short skirt ❧ Got no pride!*

MEN: *Bumpin' in the shed ❧ Bouncin' in the bed*

TOWNSPEOPLE: *Don't you know it ain't no lie...*

CHURCH LADIES, TOWNSPEOPLE & MISTER: *Shug Avery comin' to town*

CELIE: *Got about a million questions ❧ Crawling around my head ❧ What she wear? ❧ How her hair? ❧ Is she skinny? ❧ Is she stout? ❧ Must be somethin' to fuss about—*

WOMEN: *Shug Avery bring down this town!*

CHURCH MAMA: Fire and brimstone rainin' down! *Oh, she ❧ Comin,' comin'*

The men enter.

MEN: *Shug Avery heat up this town!*

CHURCH MAMA: She gonna turn into a pillar of salt! *No, no, no, no!*

CHURCH LADIES & ENSEMBLE: *Shug Avery she back in town!*

WOMEN: *Ooh, that Shug ❧ You know she no good ❧ A snake in the woods ❧ Gonna poison you*

MEN: *You don't understand ❧ What it do to a man ❧ When you in her hands ❧ And she turn that screw*

WOMEN: *Better say farewell ❧ 'Cause you're goin' to hell!*

MEN: *But a man feel swell ❧ When he in her spell*

WOMAN: *Better lock your doors!*

MEN: *Better change your drawers!*

TOGETHER: *She's coming, coming, coming, coming ❧ Shug Avery she back in town!*

The men dance.

ALL: *Shug Avery...*

Everybody sees Shug coming. She is escorted by a driver. She appears to be in control.

ALL: *She back in town!*

Shug faints into Mister's arms.

DORIS: Shug?

"Shug Avery comin' to town!"

MISTER: Baby!

Mister picks her up and exits. The Church Ladies close in, shocked at how bad Shug looks. The men follow. She still looks good to them.

JARENE: What's the matter with her?

DARLENE: She look half dead.

DORIS: *She just be catchin' flies now*

CHURCH LADIES: *She just be catchin' flies* ❧ *Now*

The women of the town continue to protest Shug's presence as the men voice their opinion.

MEN (whispering): *Shug burnin'!*

JARENE (to her husband): Get on over here!

MEN (whispering): *Shug burnin'!*

JARENE'S HUSBAND: I ain't doin' nuthin'.

WOMEN (whispering): *Shug easy*

DARLENE (to her husband): You goin' home with me.

WOMEN (whispering): *Shug easy*

DARLENE'S HUSBAND: I just seein' if everybody all right.

TOWNSPEOPLE (whispering): *Shug Avery!*

DORIS (to everyone): Ain't no business of yours where he's takin' her.

TOWNSPEOPLE: *Shug Avery...*

JARENE'S HUSBAND: Oh, I know where he takin' her.

TOWNSPEOPLE: *Shug Avery...*

JARENE: What are you doin' standin' in the street?

JARENE'S HUSBAND: I'm comin', I'm comin'.

The men and women walk offstage, still arguing about this. At Mister's house, Mister arrives holding Shug in his arms.

MISTER: Celie! Celie!

Celie opens the door for them.

SHUG: You sure is ugly!

And she faints back into Mister's arms. Church Ladies enter.

DORIS: *She got dem heebies and jeebies* ❧ *From moonshine and cheap wine* ❧ *And reefer and candy cane*

DARLENE: *Or is it the nasty relations* ❧ *From earthly sensations* ❧ *That put her in her pain?*

JARENE: *She a woman of low moral character*

ALL CHURCH LADIES: *And that's all-ll-ll-ll we got to say—*

In Mister's house, Shug lies in the bathtub, her legs hanging over the sides. Mister holds her hand.

SHUG (jerks her hand away): Turn loose my hand! I don't need no weak little boy can't say no to his daddy hanging on me. I need a man. A man!

Celie enters, standing in the doorway with a tray. Mister exits and takes out his pipe.

SHUG: And I don't want to smell no stinking pipe, neither. You hear me, Albert?

Mister stands outside the bedroom door. Celie picks up a washcloth, but stops cold, knocked out by the sight of her.

CELIE: *Got about a million tingles* ❧ *Sneakin' on up my spine* ❧ *I wash her body and it feel like I'm prayin'* ❧ *Try not to look but my eyes ain't obeyin'* ❧ *Guess I found out what all of the fuss is about* ❧ *Not like Nettie, not like Sofia* ❧ *Not like nobody else up in here* ❧ *Shug Avery*

Shug stands up nude from the tub.

SHUG: This who they talkin' about.

CELIE: I know that.

SHUG: *And everything they say is true*

So you better believe it.

CELIE: *Shug Avery*

Celie wraps Shug in a towel as she helps her out of the tub. We see Shug's nude silhouette as Celie helps to dress her. Outside the bedroom, Mister is waiting outside the bedroom door. Harpo enters.

HARPO: You think Shug come sing at the juke joint some night?

Celie combs out the knottiest, shortest, kinkiest hair she's ever seen.

MISTER: She might. But if I's you, I'd get Celie to ask her.

Inside the bedroom, Celie sits on the bed combing Shug's hair.

SHUG: Can't you hurry none?

CELIE: You got the knottiest, shortest, kinkiest hair I ever seen. You so tender-headed, I got to take my time—otherwise you be trying to slap me for hurting you.

Shug laughs.

CELIE: I'm gonna work on your head like you were my own little girl, Olivia.

Shug leans back on Celie's legs. She sighs with pleasure, then—

SHUG: The other day you say you think your sister dead. Why?

CELIE: If she alive, she write me, that's why.

SHUG: What if she been writin' you, and her letters got lost in the mail?

Shug clearly has something in mind with these questions, but decides not to go any further at this point. Outside the bedroom door, Harpo passes Ol Mister on his way up the stairs.

HARPO: What you doin' here, Grandpa?

OL MISTER: I heard my fool son got his ho back. I come to see for myself.

Harpo goes on down the steps. Ol Mister addresses Mister.

OL MISTER: Just couldn't rest til you got her in your house, could you.

Celie comes out of the bedroom.

CELIE: Ol Mister? You want a cool glass of water?

Inside the bedroom, Shug is listening.

OL MISTER: Just what is it about this Shug Avery, anyway? Even her daddy say she easy. She ain't even clean. People say she got the nasty woman disease.

On the side, Celie spits into Ol Mister's glass, twirls it around with her finger and then hands it to him. Mister sees her but doesn't say anything.

MISTER: You ain't got it in you to understand. I love Shug Avery. Always have, always will. I should have married her when I had the chance.

OL MISTER: Yeah, and throwed your life away.

MISTER: My life throwed away without her.

OL MISTER: You married Shug Avery, she woulda took you off to Memphis and what woulda happened to my farmland, huh?

MISTER: Is that all you care about, your farmland?

OL MISTER: You'd care about this land too if you was born a slave on it, like I was. You'd know what it meant to own somethin'. You'd want to pass it on to your kids, see it grow into something better, see it prosper.

MISTER (modest pride): We doin' all right.

OL MISTER: You think I raised you so you could do all right? You had chances I never had and look at you. Whole town's laughin'.

MISTER: We talkin' about Shug now? I thought we was talkin' about your farm.

OL MISTER: We talkin' about what's important here.

MISTER: To you.

OL MISTER: To a *man*.

Mister could kill him now. This charge of weakness is the end.

MISTER: To a man like you. Celie, hand Pa his hat.

Ol Mister realizes they're kicking him out.

OL MISTER: All right, then.

Ol Mister finally drinks the water, hands the glass back to Celie and leaves. After a moment:

CELIE: Next time, I'll put a little Shug Avery pee in his glass. See how he like that.

He appreciates what she's said.

Mister
Ol Mister

MISTER: That be all right with me.

Harpo comes up to the bedroom door.

HARPO: Miss Shug, I put up the signs on every tree in the county. You singin' one week from tonight. That still right?

SHUG: Long as my dress get here from Memphis, and Celie fix it by then.

HARPO (calling to his buddies): Ok, Boys. Bring it up.

CELIE: What you gone and done, Harpo?

SHUG (sees the piano): Oh my God.

The guys appear with a piano on the stairs.

HARPO: Got Miss Shug a piano to work on. If she ain't ready to sing, people tear the place down.

CELIE: We'll be ready, Harpo.

As the men begin placing the piano, Harpo goes back down the stairs.

SHUG: Right here be fine. You some strong boys. Uh-huh. Y'all come down to Harpo's and see me.

In the bedroom, Celie is working on Shug's dress.

CELIE: You gained a little weight back, but not enough, yet.

SHUG: Tell me the truth, Miss Celie. Do you mind if Albert sleep with me?

CELIE: You still love him?

SHUG: I got what you call a passion for him. He weak, I know, but he smell right to me. He make me laugh.

CELIE: And you like to sleep with him?

SHUG: I just love it. Don't you?

CELIE: I don't like it at all. Most times I pretend I ain't there. He never know the difference. Just do his business, get off, go to sleep.

SHUG (laughs): Do his business? You make it sound like he going to the toilet on you.

CELIE: That what it feel like.

SHUG: You never enjoy it ever?

CELIE: No, never. He think I'm ugly. It all right.

SHUG: No. It not all right. I had an ounce of what you got, I wouldn't have to run around shakin' my titties and waving my ass in everybody face. You not ugly. You the grace of God if us ever see it. (a moment) You don't believe me.

Shug is stricken by Celie's beauty and tenderness. She takes Celie over to the mirror.

SHUG:
Miss Celie, Miss Celie...look here. Look at yourself.

I've always been the kind of gal / That had a lot to say / I says the things that's on my mind / Too dumb to shy away / You hush my mouth and still me / With a song I never heard / I guess that means that you are just / Too beautiful for words

I've seen this life from high and low / And all that's in-between / I danced with dukes, crooned with counts / Been courted like a queen / But when I see what's in your heart / All the rest is blurred / The grace you bring into this world's / Too beautiful for words

You hide your head under your wing / Just like a little bird

Oh, don't you know you're beautiful / Too beautiful for words?

Lights close in on the two of them. Celie smiles.

Too beautiful for words

Scene Seven: The Juke

Shug gets ready to sing - and the joint is jumpin'

THE JUKE IS JUMPIN'.

HARPO (TO PIANO PLAYER): JAWBONE!

MUSIC VAMP BEGINS. HARPO ADDRESSES THE JUKE CROWD.

HARPO: ALRIGHT, Y'ALL. LET'S HEAR ONE MORE FROM THE QUEEN HONEYBEE!

HARPO & CROWD: *Shug Avery!*

HARPO: BORN RIGHT HERE, MADE IT BIG IN MEMPHIS AND COME RIGHT BACK TO SING FOR Y'ALL.

HARPO & CROWD: *Shug Avery!*

THE CROWD CHEERS AND SHUG STARTS INTO HER BIG NUMBER.

SHUG: *Now there's something 'bout good lovin' That all you ladies should know If you want to light your man on fire You better start it real slow Keep on turning up the voltage Til that man begin to glow Like you switchin' on a lightbulb Watch the juice begin to flow*

Now that I got your attention Here's what you men need to hear You want your lady racin' with you You gotta get her in gear Here's a key to rev her motor Find the spot she love the best If you don't know where it is Give her the stick, she do the rest

Push da button!

BAND & CROWD: *Push da button!*

SHUG: *Push da button!*

BAND & CROWD: *Push da button!*

SHUG: *Gotta push it If you wanna come in! Push da button!*

BAND & CROWD: *Push da button!*

SHUG: *To let your baby know It ain't no sin If you wanna feel a train a-comin' your way Baby, push da button And pull the windowshade*

Now listen all you red-hot lovers You oughta know what to do

BAND & CROWD: *You oughta know what to do*

SHUG: *There ain't nuthin' wrong with nuthin' That's right with both of you*

BAND & CROWD: *That's right with both of you*

SHUG: *So when tonight you make your lover Cry out like a lion roar Tell the neighbors your new kitty Found the cream it lookin' for!*

Push da button!

BAND & CROWD: *Push da button!*

SHUG: *Push da button!*

BAND & CROWD: *Push da button!*

SHUG: *Gotta push it If you wanna come in! Woo! Push da button*

BAND & CROWD: *Push da button!*

SHUG: *Give me somethin'...*

BAND & CROWD: *Push da button!*

SHUG: *...to let your baby know*

CROWD: *It ain't no sin*

SHUG: *Now, if you wanna feel a train A-comin' your way*

CROWD: *Woo woo*

SHUG: *Baby, push da button And pull the windowshade! Come on! Woo!*

SHUG: *Push!*

CROWD: *Pull!*

SHUG: *Push!*

CROWD: *Pull!*

DANCE SECTION

SHUG: *Push da button!*

BAND & CROWD: *Push da button!*

SHUG: *Push da button!*

BAND & CROWD: *Push da button!*

SHUG: *Gotta push it If you wanna come in! Push da button*

BAND & CROWD: *Push da button!*

SHUG: *Give me somethin'...*

BAND & CROWD: *Push da button!*

SHUG: *...To let your baby know It ain't no sin If you wanna feel a train a-comin' your way Baby, push da button And pull the windowshade!*

Push da button!

THEN SHUG AND MISTER END UP AT CELIE'S TABLE. THE CHURCH LADIES ENTER.

SOFIA: COME ON, BUSTER!

SOFIA ENTERS WITH A MAN WHO LOOKS LIKE A PRIZEFIGHTER.

Sofia walks in with Henry Broadnax

CHURCH LADIES: *Who dis? Look at Who dat? Dat So-fi-a Tell me Who dat wit her? Who dis? Look at Who dat? Dat So-fi-a Wait til Harpo see her!*

SOFIA: Would you look at what Harpo done here.

Sofia spots Celie and walks over to her table.

SOFIA: *Oooooh, Miss Celie*

Celie makes an introduction and then indicates the man Sofia has come with.

CELIE: Sofia, this here's Shug Avery.

SOFIA: Nice to meet you, m'am.

CELIE: Who that?

SOFIA: *This here is Henry Henry Broadnax*

CHURCH LADIES: *Oh, Henry!*

SOFIA: *But everybody call him Buster A prizefighter And friend of the family*

CHURCH LADIES: *Oh! Oh! Oh, Buster!*

MISTER: *Where your chirren at, Sofia?*

SOFIA: *Where your'n?*

Harpo sees Sofia and confronts her.

HARPO: *Oh no, Sofia What are you doin' here? A woman need to She need to be at home*

SOFIA: *I come to hear Miss Shug sing A woman need to have some fun Ain't that right, Miss Celie?*

HARPO: *It jes a scandless—*

CHURCH LADIES: *Scandless!*

HARPO: *Gal with five chirren Out in a juke at night*

SOFIA: *You know I got six chirren now*

HARPO & CELIE: *Six?!*

SOFIA: *Life don't stop just 'cause you leave home Ain't that right, Miss Celie?*

Celie doesn't respond. Sofia hugs Buster.

SOFIA: Buster, let's get a seat.

HARPO: Play somethin', Jawbone.

She looks at him as if to object, then he stands and extends his hand to her. The music plays as they walk toward each other. She looks at him as if to object, then he stands and extends his hand to her.

HARPO: *Let's dance*

They walk toward each other.

BUSTER: Well, that's the first time I ever been knocked down without throwin' a punch!

"Push Da Button"

The music plays as Sofia puts both arms around Harpo's neck and as soon as they touch, even we can feel the heat that is still there between them.

SOFIA: *Harpo, be nice, be nice*

Harpo begins to melt, remembering what it was like in the beginning with her. And they dance even closer.

HARPO: *So-fia, So-fi-a*

But Squeak has appeared now and spotted them.

SQUEAK: *Harpo! Who this woman?*

HARPO: You know who she is.

SQUEAK: *She best to leave you alone!*

WOMEN: Uh-oh.

SOFIA: Fine with me.

HARPO (grabs Sofia by the arm): *Baby, you don't have to go nowhere* *Hell, this is your damn house!*

SQUEAK: *What do you mean this is her house?!* *You said it was our house* *She walk away from it* *So it over now!*

CROWD: *Uh-oh*

SOFIA: Fine with me.

HARPO: *Woman, can't a man get some peace* *Dancin' with his own wife?*

SQUEAK: *Not if he my man, and not if he love me* *No, not if he my man he can't* *You hear that, bitch?*

CROWD: *Uh-oh*

Squeak and Sofia square off

Music starts, building...

CHURCH LADIES: *Her house? This is your house* *Ain't but one house, tell me whose is it?* *Her house, this is your house* *Ain't but one house, better keep him in it*

SQUEAK: You ain't nuthin' but a big old heifer.

SOFIA: Like I said, fine with me.

CHURCH LADIES: *Her house?* *This is your house* *Ain't but one—*

Squeak slaps Sofia across the head.

BUSTER & CROWD: *Uh-oh!!*

Sofia balls up her fist, draws back and punches Squeak. They roll on the ground fighting. The fight ends as Sofia punches Squeak and knocks her out. The music stops. Harpo pulls Sofia off of Squeak.

HARPO (to Sofia): I don't allow no fightin' in here.

SOFIA: She slap me, everybody see that.

HARPO: And you knock her out like she a man. Take Sofia home, Buster.

Sofia collects her dignity. Buster walks away with Sofia. Celie watches as Sofia and Buster exit. Shug takes Celie's hand and exits. Harpo picks Squeak up and carries her off.

The bedroom. Shug and Celie enter laughing about the night. They fall onto the bed.

CELIE: Harpo make a lot of money if you stay here and sing.

SHUG: Yeah, but now you got me feelin' so much better, I got to get back on the road, make some money, you know.

CELIE: I don't want you to go. Mister beat me when you're not here.

SHUG: What he beat you for?

CELIE: For being me and not you. Please don't go. (a moment) Everybody gone now. My mama. My kids. My Nettie. Even Sofia.

SHUG: But Sofia already back, big as life. She not done with Harpo from what I seen tonight, uh-uh.

CELIE: When you have to go?

SHUG: In the morning. But I'll be back too in a month or so. You'll see.

CELIE: You gone an hour it feel like a year to me.

SHUG: I'll be back. Nobody ever love me like you.

THEY ARE SURPRISED BY WHAT SHUG HAS SAID. SHUG LAUGHS.

SHUG: DAMN, GIRL.

SHUG KISSES HER.

CELIE: *Is that me who's floating away? Lifted up to the clouds by a kiss Never felt nothin' like this*

SHUG: *Is that me I don't recognize? Love's the one thing I knew all about I had it all figured out*

CELIE: *But what about trust?*

SHUG: *What about trust?*

CELIE: *What about tenderness?*

SHUG: *Tenderness?*

CELIE & SHUG: *What about tears when I'm happy? What about wings when I fall? I want you to be A story for me That I can believe in forever*

CELIE: *So what about*

SHUG: *What about*

CELIE & SHUG: *Love?*

CELIE & SHUG: *Will you be my light in the storm? Will I see a new world in your eyes? With you my whole spirit rise*

CELIE: *And what about hope?*

SHUG: *What about hope?*

CELIE: *What about joy?*

SHUG: *What about joy?*

CELIE & SHUG: *What about tears when I'm happy? What about wings when I fall? I want you to be A story for me That I can believe in forever*

SHUG: *So what about*

"What about love?"

CELIE: *What about*

SHUG: *What about*

CELIE: *What about*

CELIE & SHUG: *Love?*

CELIE: *What about*

SHUG: *What about*

CELIE: *What about*

SHUG: *What about*

CELIE: *What about love?...*

SHUG: *You and me*

CELIE: *Ah—*

SHUG: *You and me*

CELIE: *You and me*

SHUG: *You and me, oh*

CELIE: *La la la*

SHUG: *Sent to me*

CELIE: *What about*

SHUG: *La la What about*

CELIE: *What about*

SHUG: *Love?*

CELIE: *Love?*

SHUG GOES AND GETS A LETTER. WE FEEL THE RISK SHE IS TAKING.

SHUG: NOW LOOK HERE. I FOUND A BUNCH OF MAIL FOR YOU THAT ALBERT'S BEEN HIDIN'. IT'S MOSTLY JUNK, BUT THERE'S A WHOLE PILE OF LETTERS FROM SOMEBODY IN AFRICA, GOIN' BY THE STAMPS. LIKE THIS ONE.

SHUG HANDS HER THE LETTER. CELIE TAKES IT. INSTANTLY SHE FEELS THE PRESENCE OF NETTIE IN THE LETTER. SHE RUBS THE ENVELOPE, THEN RUBS THE STAMPS AND LOOKS AT THE WRITING.

CELIE: IT'S FROM NETTIE!

NETTIE STEPS ONSTAGE, IN HER WHITE DRESS IN CELIE'S MEMORY.

NETTIE: DEAR CELIE, I KNOW YOU THINK I AM DEAD. BUT I AM NOT. I'VE BEEN WRITING TO YOU EVERY WEEK ALL THESE YEARS BUT I GUESS YOU DIDN'T GET ANY MY LETTERS BECAUSE YOU HAVEN'T WRITTEN BACK.

CELIE: SHE'S ALIVE.

NETTIE: YOU PROBABLY WON'T GET THIS ONE EITHER, 'CAUSE I'M SURE MISTER IS STILL THE ONLY ONE TO TAKE MAIL OUT OF THE BOX. BUT IF YOU DO, ONE THING I WANT YOU TO KNOW, I LOVE YOU, AND I AM NOT DEAD.

MUSIC COMES UP UNDER AS CELIE CLUTCHES A LETTER TO HER HEART.

CELIE: NETTIE'S ALIVE! SHE'S ALIVE!

END OF THE ACT.

Act Two · Scene One · Africa / Sofia

The African women first welcome Nettie –

It is one moment after the end of Act 1. Shug and Celie are with Nettie's letters.

SHUG: Look, how many letters there are! There must be hundreds.

CELIE: I've walked over these for years!

MISTER (offstage): Celie!!!

SHUG: I'll go entertain Albert, and you keep reading your letters.

Mister enters. Shug goes to meet him.

MISTER: *Shug Avery!*

SHUG: *My daddy say I'm easy…*

MISTER: *That's what I'm talkin' about*

SHUG: *But I'm misunderstood* I need me a drink.

Laughing and kissing, Mister and Shug exit.

Celie can feel Nettie calling to her through the letters, a cascade of sound.

PART 1
CELIE FINDS NETTIE

NETTIE: *Dear Celie, dear Celie, dear Celie*

CELIE: Nettie!

As Celie opens the first letter, Nettie appears.

NETTIE: *Dear Celie, oh, I love you ~ Years go by and still you're with me ~ All we share is one big sky ~ I pray for your reply*

I teach your children ABCs ~ For my missionary family ~ These babies sent by God are yours

NETTIE & CELIE: *Adam and Olivia alive, alive!*

We hear the sound of a horn as the boat pulls into the harbor.

PART 2
CELIE & NETTIE MEET THE AFRICANS

Celie and Nettie meet the Africans. The people of the village come onstage as Nettie stands with the children.

NETTIE: *I vibrated like a bell ~ When I saw the African coast ~ And we kneeled down and thanked God*

CELIE: *Thank God*

NETTIE & CELIE: *Thank God*

NETTIE: *For letting us see the land where our ~ Mothers and fathers died*

NETTIE & CELIE: *African homeland, homeland ~ Land of my people, people*

ALL: *People*

NETTIE: We're going to be working with a tribe called the Olinka.

The Africans move toward them. Nettie listens carefully as the Chief speaks.

CHIEF: Ah ma wha dee wo yo yo…

TRIBE: Yea

NETTIE: They didn't know when the ship would come.

CHIEF: Eye ya way oh moomsa day.

TRIBE: Mmm. Mmm mm

NETTIE: So they waited for two weeks at the dock.

CHIEF: My why ya ashto magwa…

NETTIE: And they took us to their village.

PART 3
JOURNEY TO THE VILLAGE

The Africans lead Nettie and Celie and the kids to the village. The Chief and Villagers begin the chant, then it's picked up by Nettie, and finally by Celie and the kids.

CHIEF: *Linga*

VILLAGERS: *Linga*

CHIEF: *Oba*

VILLAGERS: *Oba*

CHIEF: *Batuwanga*

MEN: *Ada doon da yay*

CHIEF: *Oba*

VILLAGERS: *Linga*

CHIEF: *Oba*

VILLAGERS: *Oba*

CHIEF: *Batuwanga*

MEN: *Ada doon da yay*

CHIEF & VILLAGERS: *Linga*

NETTIE: *Linga*

Celie dreams of holding her children

CHIEF & VILLAGERS: *Oba*

NETTIE: *Oba*

CHIEF & VILLAGERS: *Batuwanga*

NETTIE: *Ada doon da yay*

THE VILLAGERS DANCE AS NETTIE REPEATS AND TRANSLATES AS CELIE AND THE KIDS JOIN THE DANCE.

CHIEF/VILLAGERS/CELIE/KIDS: *Linga*

NETTIE: *We are*

CHIEF/VILLAGERS/CELIE/KIDS: *Oba*

NETTIE: *Happy*

NETTIE: *At the center ◦ Of the universe*

CHIEF/VILLAGERS/CELIE/KIDS: *Linga*

NETTIE: *We are*

CHIEF/VILLAGERS/CELIE/KIDS: *Oba*

NETTIE: *Happy ◦ At the center ◦ Of the universe*

THE DANCE CONTINUES AS THE DRUMBEAT CHANGES.

CHIEF & VILLAGERS: *Oh dee dee oo day oo day oo dadoo day doo da day ◦ Oh dee dee oo day oo day oo dadoo day doo da day ◦ Oh yoo doh doo day ay ay*

WOMEN: *Oh yo oon daday*

CHIEF & VILLAGERS: *Oh yoo doh doo day ay ay ◦ Oh yoo doh doo day ay ay*

WOMEN: *Oh yo oon daday*

CHIEF & VILLAGERS: *Oh yoo doh doo day ay ay*

NETTIE IS OVERCOME NOW WITH THE BEAUTY OF THESE PEOPLE.

CHIEF & VILLAGERS: *Oh dee dee oo day oo day oo dadu day doo da day ◦ Oh yoo doh doo day ay ay*

WOMEN: *Oh yo oon daday*

CHIEF & VILLAGERS: *Oh yoo doh doo day ay ay ◦ Oh yoo doh doo day ay ay*

WOMEN: *Eeleeyah ooday*

CHIEF & VILLAGERS: *Oh yoo doh doo day ay ay*

THEY HAVE ARRIVED NOW AT THE VILLAGE. THE CHIEF GIVES A GESTURE OF WELCOME. CELIE WATCHES THE WELCOME DANCE. NETTIE WALKS THROUGH THE VILLAGERS WITH ADAM AND OLIVIA.

NETTIE: *It was like black seeing black ◦ For the first time ◦ Shiny blue-black people looking real fine ◦ In brilliant blue robes ◦ That fly on the wind ◦ Like a beautiful quilt ◦ Stitched together by friends*

CELIE JOINS NETTIE.

CELIE: *You could put everything I knew in ◦ A thimble ◦ What we're taught to be ◦ Don't resemble ◦ The kings and queens who for thousands of years ◦ Ruled magnificent cities ◦ Washed away by tears*

PART 4

DAILY LIFE

THE WOMEN RUN UPSTAGE AS THE CHIEF CALLS OUT TO THE HUNTERS.

THE CHIEF: *Ah too bah yah!*

THE HUNT DRUMS BEGIN.

THE CHIEF: AH TOO BAH YAHHHH!

THE HUNTERS DANCE AS THE CHIEF LOOKS OUT ON THE VILLAGE ADMIRING ITS PROSPERITY. THE HUNT DRUMS END. THE WOMEN SING AS THEY BEGIN THEIR DAY.

WOMEN, CELIE & NETTIE: *Ee yea ahn ya ◦ Ee yea ahn ya ◦ Ee yea ahn ya ◦ Ee yea ahn ya oh*

THE DRUMS AND HUNTERS' DANCE GETS MORE INTENSE. THE WOMEN, NETTIE, AND CELIE REPRISE THEIR CHANT CELEBRATING THE HUNT.

WOMEN, CELIE & NETTIE: *Ee yea ahn ya ~ Ee yea ahn ya ~ Ee yea ahn ya ~ Ee yea ahn ya oh*

JUST AS THE SONG REACHES ITS CELEBRATORY CLIMAX WE HEAR MISTER FIRST, THEN SEE HIM CALLING FOR CELIE. AS SHE SEES HIM, AFRICA DISAPPEARS.

MISTER: CELIE!

FINAL DRUMBEATS AS SHE SEES HIM, AND AFRICA DISAPPEARS.

MISTER: CELIE!

CELIE LOOKS UP, TERRIFIED. SHE HAS NO IDEA WHERE SHE IS, OR HOW LONG SHE HAS BEEN READING LETTERS. SHE HIDES THE LETTERS AND SITS. MISTER ENTERS.

MISTER: WHAT YOU DOIN'?

CELIE: NUTHIN'.

MISTER: I AIN'T NEVER SEEN YOU JUST SIT.

CELIE: HOW IT LOOK?

SHUG ENTERS.

SHUG: GOOD MORNING.

CELIE: Y'ALL WANT SOME BREAKFAST?

SHUG: WISH I COULD BUT I GOT TO GO. TAKE THIS ON OUT TO THE CAR.

MISTER EXITS WITH SUITCASE.

CELIE: SOON AS HE GET BACK FROM TOWN, I'M GON KILL HIM.

SHUG: NO. BIBLE SAY DON'T KILL.

CELIE: NO. I THINK I FEEL BETTER IF I KILL HIM.

SHUG: NO YOU WON'T. NOBODY FEEL BETTER FOR KILLING NOTHING. THINK OF ME. THINK OF NETTIE. YOU JUST FINISH READIN' YOUR LETTERS.

SHUG EMBRACES HER, GIVES HER A KISS, AND LEAVES.

CELIE: GOODBYE.

PART 5

AFRICA TURNS ON NETTIE

THE COLORS ARE DARKER NOW, THERE IS SOME NEW DANGER PRESENT. CELIE IS SEEING A CHANGED AFRICA. CELIE GRABS THE FIRST LETTER SHE CAN FIND.

CELIE: *My Nettie—*

SHE OPENS IT. AS NETTIE ENTERS WITH THE AFRICAN WOMEN AND CHILDREN SINGING.

NETTIE: DEAR CELIE,

CHILDREN SING UNDER AS NETTIE CONTINUES.

OLINKA CHILDREN: *Hey nyah mah ko weem bay ~ Oh ko chee yam way ~ Ah yo yah yo...eee! ~ Dwee yum doo way ~ Dah see ma doe ya ya ~ Oh bo jah ma ma ~ Ah yo yah yo...eeee! ~ Dwee yum doo way*

NETTIE: I'VE BEEN TEACHING THE OLINKA TO READ. BUT SOME OF THE WOMEN HAVE BECOME VERY SUSPICIOUS OF ME BECAUSE GIRLS HAVE NEVER BEEN TAUGHT TO READ HERE. GIRLS HAVE NEVER BEEN TAUGHT ANYTHING AT ALL. I DON'T UNDERSTAND EVERYTHING THEY'RE SAYING, BUT WHAT IT SOUNDS LIKE TO ME IS—

The chief

AND THE MUSICAL TONE CHANGES AS THREE AFRICAN WIVES ENTER AND ADDRESS NETTIE.

AFRICAN WIVES: *What this mess you been preachin'? ~ Why you tryin' to change us?*

NETTIE: THEY THINK I SHOULD BE MARRIED.

AFRICAN WIVES (NODDING IN AGREEMENT): *Whoop! ~ Girl ain't nothing with no man ~ Why you makin' a big fuss? ~ Whoop! ~ Need a husband and children ~ Or you're gonna be nothing*

NETTIE TURNS TO FACE THE WOMEN.

NETTIE: *I am nobody's mother ~ But I am somebody*

AFRICAN WIVES: *Girls don't need education*

NETTIE: *Sound like the white folks back home*

AFRICAN WIVES: *Best be knowing your station*

Nettie is caught in an African war

NETTIE GRABS OLIVIA AND HOLDS HER CLOSE.

NETTIE & CELIE: BUT NOT MY OLIVIA!

AFRICAN WIVES: *Hmmmmmmm*

THE AFRICAN WIVES EXIT.

PART 6

THE WAR

THE SOUNDS OF WAR FILL THE STAGE. AN AFRICAN MAN RUNS INTO THE VILLAGE WITH NEWS OF WAR.

MAN: MATANG GAAAAAAA!

SOUND OF AN EXPLOSION.

CELIE: NETTIE!

AFRICAN MEN COME ON PREPARING FOR WAR. CELIE RUNS INTO THE SCENE, BUT SHE CAN'T FIND NETTIE IN THESE PREPARATIONS.

NETTIE: ADAM! OLIVIA!

NETTIE LOOKS FOR THE CHILDREN AS SHE SPEAKS HER LETTER TO CELIE.

NETTIE: CELIE. THE WHITE SOLDIERS CAME, BURNING OUR VILLAGE, AND VILLAGES ALL AROUND US.

ADAM JOINS THE MEN TO FIGHT

CELIE: NO, ADAM! YOU'RE TOO YOUNG. YOU DON'T EVEN KNOW WHAT YOU'RE FIGHTING ABOUT. NO!

CELIE CONTINUES TO LOOK FOR NETTIE.

CELIE: NETTIE!

Nettie

CELIE WALKS AMONG THE FIGHTERS, BUT SHE CAN'T FIND NETTIE OR THE CHILDREN.

CELIE: NETTIE!

NETTIE, HOLDING ADAM AND OLIVIA, STAYS WITH THE AFRICAN WOMEN AS THEY BEGIN TO SUFFER THE EFFECTS OF THE FIGHTING. ONE BY ONE, THE MEN RETURN, DEFEATED OR KILLED. AS THE CONFUSION INCREASES, CELIE STILL CAN'T FIND NETTIE. SHE IS AS LOST AS ALL OF THEM.

PART 7

THE DESTRUCTION

NOW WE SEE THE DESTRUCTION OF THE PEOPLE. WOMEN WATCH IN HORROR. PUSHED BACK FROM THEIR LAND. RECOGNIZING THEIR LIFE IS OVER. MEN RETURNING FROM FIGHTING. NETTIE DISAPPEARS. CELIE WANDERS WITHOUT ANY HOPE OF FINDING NETTIE. THEN, ANOTHER SCENE COMES IN TO TAKE UP THE SPACE LEFT BY THE RETREATING AFRICANS.

HARPO ENTERS LOOKING FOR CELIE.

HARPO: MISS CELIE!

CELIE HEARS HIM AND GOES TOWARD THE VOICE.

CELIE: HARPO?

HARPO RUNS THROUGH AFRICA LOOKING FOR CELIE.

HARPO: MISS CELIE!

CELIE: WHAT YOU NEED, HARPO?

THE AFRICAN WOMEN ARE TRYING TO CARE FOR THE MEN. TRYING TO SUPPORT EACH OTHER. THEY RETREAT AND WATCH IN HORROR AS THE EUROPEANS DESTROY THEIR LAND.

HARPO: IT'S ABOUT SOFIA!

SOFIA APPEARS.

SOFIA: COME ON, Y'ALL. LET'S GET OUR SHOPPING DONE AND GET OUTTA HERE. LESS TIME I SPEND LOOKING AT THESE WHITE FOLKS, THE BETTER I FEEL.

As the African exodus continues...

HARPO: They beat her up!

CELIE: Who did?

HARPO: The mayor's men did. Sofia was in town shoppin' and the mayor's wife come up, said Sofia's children was so clean, ask Sofia if she wanted to be her maid, keep her house as clean as Sofia children. Sofia say

SOFIA: Hell no!

HARPO: The mayor grab Sofia, say what you say to Miss Millie? Sofia say

SOFIA: Hell no.

HARPO: Buster try to stop her, but the mayor call his men—

SOFIA: Take Henrietta home, Buster. Buster!!!!

As Sofia is beaten up, Harpo continues

HARPO: Sofia fought back, but they got her in jail now. And they beatin' her up every day. They blind her in one eye. She can't talk. But if you go down there, they let you clean her up.

CELIE: They let me in?

HARPO: Please, Miss Celie. I'll take you. Will you go, Miss Celie?

CELIE: You take me, I'll go.

As Harpo explains what has happened, Celie feels the pull of both these things—the horror of Africa and the horror of what has happened to Sofia.

As the Olinka retreat continues, the retreating people seem both to be mourning their own loss, and the loss of Sofia. A guard takes Sofia to jail.

Nettie enters with Adam and Olivia.

NETTIE: Our village was destroyed by the soldiers, so now we have walked with so many other refugees to a tent camp across the border. I don't know how I will mail this letter.

PART 8
THE END

NETTIE: *We walk away from this ravaged land ◦ With courage deep in our hearts ◦ To face the unknown*

Some of the people are angry and want to go back.

NETTIE & OLINKA: *Together*

One of the women does a mourning dance saying goodbye to the land.

NETTIE: *We'll find a place where we can be ◦ Where spirit rise and soul is free ◦ Oh people*

OLINKA: *Oon day oondala*

NETTIE: *My people*

OLINKA: *Oon day oondala*

Nettie joins the retreating Olinka and speaks to Celie across the divide of time and space.

NETTIE: I have faith that God will let us see each other again before we die. And you must have faith too, Celie. I only hope when that day comes, we are not too old to recognize each other.

ALL: *We walk away ◦ Ahummmmmm ◦ We walk away ◦ Ahummmmmm*

Nettie takes the children's hands and joins the people walking.

NETTIE: Adam and Olivia know that you are their mother. Don't you worry about them. You just...take care of things there. We'll get home somehow. Your sister,

CELIE: Nettie.

Celie walks toward the jail. The guard brings Sofia into the cell.

At the jail, Sofia sits in her cell, alone, badly beaten. The guard escorts Celie into the cell and leaves. Celie sees Sofia, and gasps. Sofia doesn't even look up.

CELIE: Sofia. It's me, Celie. Can you hear me? I come to...to see if I can do anything for you.

She puts some water on a cloth.

A bruised and battered Sofia

CELIE: This water might feel a little cold, but it gon take down some of that swelling. I see a couple places could use a little dab of alcohol on 'em, but you tell me if I'm hurtin' you now, all right? (Trying to lighten up) And if you got any ideas how I'm gon tame your hair, you tell me them too.

Sofia manages to move one hand toward Celie. Celie wraps her arms around Sofia and rocks her like she was a little baby. When Sofia still doesn't respond, Celie tries to think of something else to take Sofia's mind off her pain.

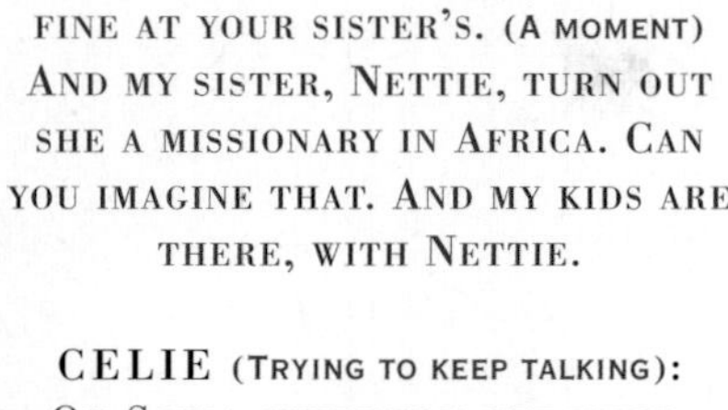

CELIE: Your kids are all doin' fine at your sister's. (A moment) And my sister, Nettie, turn out she a missionary in Africa. Can you imagine that. And my kids are there, with Nettie.

CELIE (Trying to keep talking): Oh Sofia, when you get home, and Nettie get home, us gon have a big picnic, all of us and all of our kids.

The guard enters.

GUARD: Miss Celie.

CELIE: Sofia not safe in here.

GUARD: Yeah, but I come to let her out right now.

CELIE: Right now?

GUARD: The mayor's wife, they say she feel a little bit responsible for what happened, so she talk the judge into releasin' Sofia into her custody.

CELIE: Into her custody?

GUARD: Sofia gonna be her maid after all.

CELIE: No!

GUARD (To Sofia): Come on, girl.

Celie watches as Sofia is led away by the guard. Celie spins around. Harpo appears. He takes her arm.

HARPO: You all right, Miss Celie? I appreciate what you done.

CELIE: You be glad you ain't seen what they done to her, Harpo. They kept her alive just enough so she could still wash they floor.

HARPO: You best be quiet now, til us get out of here.

The guard comes around.

HARPO: Don't want you to end up in jail too.

GUARD: Havin' some trouble there?

HARPO: No, sir. I got it.

The guard exits. Celie is so mad now, she's shaking. He holds onto her as tight as he can.

CELIE: Let go of me, Harpo.

HARPO: Not till us get outside.

Harpo comforts her.

HARPO (A moment): I stay right with you til you feel better. Then, I'll take you home.

CELIE: No. I want to walk.

Harpo exits. Celie walks downstage. She takes off her scarf to reveal her hair is now gray.

CELIE: Dear Nettie, I hope this letter finds you wherever you are. Things hard here. People always makin' things worse for each other. My only joy hearin' from you, thinkin' 'bout you. Now I know you're alive, I'm writin' ever day and walk into town to mail 'em, no matter what else happen, even if all my letters pile up at the door of Africa, I keep writin'. I love you. Your sister...

"You be glad you ain't seen what they done to her, Harpo

Scene Two: Shug home

Celie meets Grady for the first time

It is 1937, the day before Easter. Celie is 42 now. A car horn honks. Mister enters from the house.

MISTER: Celie! Look who it is! Shug done come home for Easter!

CELIE: I see that.

Shug runs to Celie.

SHUG: Celie! Celie! Hello, Albert. Celie! I want you to meet somebody.

Grady enters and goes to celie

GRADY: Hello, Albert. Miss Celie. I heard so much about the two of you, I feel like family already.

SHUG: This Grady. My husband.

CELIE: Your husband.

MISTER: How long you been married?

Shug points to a beautiful car sitting offstage.

SHUG: About a week. And this is my wedding present to us. First thing we done is drive it here to see you.

CELIE: Y'all want some ice tea?

Shug takes Celie's arm.

SHUG: Miss Celie. Us two married ladies now. And hungry. Grady. Go make us some eggs and onions. I need to stretch my legs. Celie and I got some catching up to do.

MISTER (To Grady): I'm gon have some corn liquor if you want some.

Shug and Celie walk out into the fields. Celie is very distant.

SHUG: You got you a new hat for Easter?

CELIE: No.

SHUG: You find any more letters from Nettie? How they doin' over there in Africa?

Celie doesn't respond.

SHUG: I never seen you like this, Celie. You not excited about Easter?

CELIE: Easter mean nuthin' to me. I prayed to God my whole life and what he done? Nuthin'. My Nettie lost in Africa. Sofia nearly dead. Mister nuthin' but—

SHUG: I got to get you out of here.

CELIE: I can't never leave Mister and you know it.

SHUG: What do you think we been talking about. God want us to be happy, Celie. Want us to love each other, help each other—

CELIE: God forgot about me!

SHUG: Celie. God not some gloomy old man like the pictures you've seen of him. God not a man at all.

Shug begins singing, but easily, more like these are just her thoughts with a little music underneath.

SHUG: *God is inside you and every-*
one else ◦ That was or ever will be ◦
We come into this world with God ◦
But only them that look inside, find it

God is the flowers and everything else
◦ That was or ever will be ◦ And
when you feel the truth so real ◦
And when you love the way you feel,
you've found it

Just as sure as moonlight bless the
night ◦ Like a blade of corn ◦
Like a honeybee ◦ Like a waterfall ◦
All a part of me ◦ Like the color
purple ◦ Where do it come from? ◦
Open up your eyes ◦ Look what
God has done

Celie turns away. This is not what she wants to hear.

CELIE: You better go back. Your husband probably wonderin' where you are.

SHUG: Where do you want to be, Celie?

CELIE: With you.

SHUG: All right then.

CELIE: God gon take me to live with you?

SHUG: Come on.

This idea makes them both happy, they take hands and walk through the fields as the sun goes down as the last line of verse melody plays as underscore.

Scene Three: Easter dinner

Easter dinner, but Sofia's got no appetite

The sun comes up.

The Church Ladies are shopping for Easter hats.

DARLENE: *That's such a lovely hat* ~ *A fine chapeau*

JARENE: *Your style is so down pat* ~ *Your pedigree shows*

DORIS: *Those flowers look so real* ~ *Fresh Easter bloom*

JARENE: *You got that vamp appeal*

DARLENE: *I heard about that Shug Avery* ~ *Heard about that Shug Avery* ~ *Heard about that Shug Avery* ~ *Heard about that Hi yella* ~ *And*

JARENE: *She wit some yella man Hmph!* ~ *She wit some yella man Hmph!* ~ *She wit some yella man* ~ *Hi yella* ~ *Hi yella* ~ *Hi yella* ~ *Who hootchie-kootchin'* ~ *Wit who?* ~ *Who hootchie-kootchin'* ~ *Wit who?*

DORIS: *He got a really* ~ *Lonnng Car* ~ *He got a really big car* ~ *Hi yella* ~ *Hi yella* ~ *Hi yella* ~ *What about po' chile Celie?* ~ *What about po'* ~ *Po' chile Celie?* ~ *What about po'*

CHURCH LADIES: *Mister gon moochie wit two!* ~ *Scandless!* ~ *Who hootchie kootchin' wit who?*

Inside Mister's house

The dining room appears at the end of Easter dinner. In the dining room, Mister, Ol Mister, Harpo, Grady, and Sofia sit around the table with the children. Sofia looks a lot older, her hair is streaked with gray. Shug leans against the wall by the window, smoking and looking fabulous. Squeak goes around the table pouring tea. Celie, wearing her hat and her apron, stands at the sideboard, dishing up the last piece of cake. A ham picked practically clean sits on the other end of the sideboard. Grady pushes back from the table.

GRADY: Miss Celie, that was a fine Easter dinner. Best potatoes I ever put in my mouth. If I could, I would loosen my belt, sit right down, and eat it all over again.

CELIE: There's one more piece of caramel cake if anybody wants it.

Harpo senses the tension in the room and tries to change the subject.

HARPO: Sofia, we sure glad to have you back home. Are you sure you don't want nuthin' to eat?

SOFIA (Mumbles): I don't know.

MISTER: Come on, Grady, Pa. Let's go outside so Celie can clean up this mess.

SHUG: Just hold your horses, Albert. I got something to say and I might as well say it now. Grady and me is leaving today and Celie is coming with us.

MISTER: She what?

SHUG: Celie's comin' to Memphis to live with me and Grady.

MISTER: She is not. (To Celie) What's wrong with you?

CELIE (A moment, then): You a low down dog is what's wrong. It's time for me to leave you and enter into creation.

MISTER: Over my dead—

CELIE: Your dead body be just the welcome mat I need.

MISTER (Shocked): You talkin' crazy.

CELIE (More to the rest of them): You took my sister Nettie away from me, you hid her letters for all these years, and she was the only person love me in the whole world. (To them) But my Nettie alive in Africa, and my children with Nettie in Africa, and when they come home, all us together gon whup your ass.

Mister laughs. Sofia looks up. Harpo tries to appease her.

HARPO: Miss Celie, let's just—

CELIE: I'm done bein' nice, Harpo. Your daddy made my life a hell on earth. He ain't nothing but some dead horse's shit.

Suddenly, Sofia comes to life and laughs.

OL MISTER (About Sofia): Look who just come back from the grave.

SOFIA: Dead horse's shit. Oh yes, Sofia home now. Pass me them peas, Harpo.

HARPO: I got six chirren with this crazy woman.

SOFIA: Five.

Squeak and Shug laugh now. Celie takes off her apron.

MISTER: What will people say, you running off like you don't have a house to look after?

SHUG: Why any woman give a shit what people think is a mystery to me.

This makes Sofia laugh even harder.

MISTER: You're not getting a penny from me, Celie. Not one thin dime.

CELIE: Did I ever ask you for money? I never asked you for nothing. Not even for your sorry hand in marriage.

SHUG: Come on, Celie. Let's just get out of here. Sofia take care this.

SOFIA: Oh yes. Sofia born to take care this.

Celie's curse

SQUEAK: I want to go with Celie and Shug.

HARPO: And do what?

SQUEAK: I want to sing.

MISTER: You better stop her, Harpo. You ain't my boy letting some girl talk to you like that.

HARPO: She want to sing, Pa.

SQUEAK: I'm goin' to Memphis! And I'm gon sing.

SHUG: Come on, Celie.

They start to leave.

MISTER (To Celie): You'll be back. Shug got talent. And looks. All you fit to do is be Shug's maid. Take out her slop-jar and maybe cook her food. You not that good a cook either.

CELIE: You rotten—

Celie grabs the knife off the sideboard and lunges at him. Shug comes in between them, Grabs Celie and holds onto her. Shug takes the knife from Celie.

CELIE: I curse you, Mister.

MISTER: Curse me?

CELIE: Until you do right by me, everything and everyone you touch will crumble, everything you even dream will fail.

MISTER: You can't curse nobody. You black, you poor, you ugly, you a woman. I shoulda just locked you up. Just let you out to work.

CELIE:
I may be poor — I may be black —
I may be ugly — But I'm here!

SHUG: Come on, Celie. Let's get your things. Grady. Get the car.

Music continues as Shug, Celie and Squeak go on out the door. The men are in shock. Sofia laughs and laughs. Ol Mister leaves.

Harpo and Sofia are alone. A moment.

SOFIA: How come you didn't marry that Squeak?

HARPO: Cause you still my wife, I guess.

SOFIA: That's a good reason.

HARPO: You gon live at your sister's?

SOFIA: Maybe.

HARPO (Smiles): I built a coupla new rooms on the back of the juke joint. You could live there.

Mister scoffs

Sofia leaves.

SOFIA: It my house anyway.

Harpo goes after her.

HARPO: Would you mind if I slept on the porch?

Scene Four: Mister in the Road

"Nuthin' I say gon change people mind about me"

In the night: Lightning strikes, wind blows, and terrible thunder is heard. Mister's house is seen in the darkness. Mister's voice is heard.

MISTER: No! No! Leave me alone! Get out of—get out! No! Leave me alone you—no! Goddamn bats get out of my—! No! Stop! Get away from me! Ow! Help!!!!!

He screams and runs out of the house, more lightning and thunder. Mister falls down.

On the road. It's daytime. Mister is lying in the middle of the road. People begin to walk by, looking at him. He can sense their disapproval.

MISTER: What you lookin' at? Bunch of damn fools.

Field hands turn away. They don't hear his responses.

DORIS: He always been cruel.

MISTER: Celie cursed me!

DARLENE: He never cared for nuthin'.

MISTER: There's bats in my house—

JARENE: Treat everybody like animals.
Treat animals like dirt.

FIELD HANDS: And it was us took care of the dirt, or he wouldn't even have that left.

MISTER: I don't have to stay here, worthless town. I can walk right down this road. By myself. Never see nobody I know ever again.

Nobody to put up with — Nobody to mess with me — Nobody to push me around — Nobody to tell me what to do — Nobody to expect somethin' of me — Nobody to tell me who I am and who I ain't

Nobody!

FIELD HANDS: He got nobody to blame but himself.

MISTER: *I got plenty to blame — My daddy beat me — For my own good he say — My first wife got kilt — When she run away — My kids is all fools — My crops is all dead — Only woman I love — Won't lay in my bed — A black man's life — Can't get any worse — Less he wastin' away — Under Miss Celie's curse — So tell me how a man do good when all he know is bad?*

Harpo appears. He goes over to Mister.

HARPO: Daddy. What you doin' in the road? People tell me you been standin' out here all day talking to yourself.

MISTER: Fool son.

HARPO: Let's get you home.

MISTER: *Harpo happy — What right he got to be happy? — Wife leave, girlfriend leave him too — His mama die in his arms — Somebody tell me — How he keep findin' — So much good from so much bad?*

Sofia comes on with a load of something, Henrietta walking alongside her.

HARPO: Sofia, let me get that for you.

MISTER: *His wife come back — His business fine — Everyone say Harpo shine*

SOFIA: Thank you, Harpo.

MISTER: *For all they been through — They do just fine*

Harpo picks Henrietta up.

HARPO: Come on, you sweet girl, I'll carry you too. (Turning to Pa) You want any peace, you gotta make things right with Celie like she said.

MISTER: *Nuthin' I say gon change people — Mind about me*

HARPO: You got to give back any other Nettie letters you got.

SOFIA: Come on, Harpo. Let's go home.

MISTER: *Ain't gon be nothin' I say — Gon be somethin' I do — Maybe all my good lie ahead of me*

HARPO: You all right, Pa?

Harpo reaches out his hand. Mister takes it and squeezes it. Harpo, Sofia, and Henrietta leave.

MISTER: *Ain't gon be nuthin' I say
Gon be somethin' I do
Maybe everything I do*

Scene Five: Letter Scene

Celie gets the call that her Pa is dead

All the ladies love Miss Celie's pants

It is 1943. Celie enters with a suitcase, arriving at Shug's house. She speaks her letter to Nettie.

CELIE: Dear Nettie, Us never seen anything as beautiful as Shug Avery house. It's big and pink and look sort of like a barn. Cept where you would put hay, Shug got bedrooms and toilets and a big ballroom where she and her band sometime work. (A moment) My bedroom looks out over the creek.

Shug enters carrying a cup of coffee and the newspapers and wearing a knockout robe, untied, with not much on underneath. She kisses Celie.

SHUG (Indicating the newspaper): People in the newspaper insane, Celie.

Celie continues her letter.

CELIE: Coupla months ago, Shug come back from a road trip, all bloated from eatin' bad food and she wanted me to make her some pants that would fit no matter what size she was.

SHUG: Everybody gonna want some of these, you know that.

CELIE (Showing Shug): And see here, you can bunch up the bottoms if you want to wear 'em when you singin'. They almost look like a dress.

SHUG: How'd I ever live before you?

The phone rings—Shug starts admiring herself in the mirror. A young woman appears on the other side of the stage. She is distraught, but cute.

CELIE: Hello?

DAISY: Miss Celie, it's Daisy. Alphonso wife. I call to tell you Alphonso dead, Miss Celie.

CELIE: Alphonso dead?

DAISY: Alphonso dead.

CELIE & SHUG: Who that?

Shug laughs, Celie throws her another pair of pants to try as she listens on the phone.

SHUG: This a good color for me.

CELIE (Whispers to Shug): It's Pa. He dead.

SHUG: Good.

Celie continues to listen to Daisy, and pass the information along to Shug.

CELIE (Whispers): Only he not my real Pa, she say. He just the man move in with Mama after my real Pa was lynch.

Shug admiring herself more.

SHUG: I want another pair like this in shiny red.

CELIE (Covers the mouthpiece): But the house still belong to real Pa,

SHUG (Not listening): What house?

CELIE: House I grew up in. Belong to me and Nettie now. And there's the store too. (Suddenly angry, into the phone) Well I don't want it. I was rape in that house from the time I was 12 years old.

SHUG: What you talkin' 'bout you don't want a house? Your real daddy left it for you. That dog of a step Pa just a bad odor passing through. Gimme that. (Takes the phone) Celie want that house. And the store too! And she comin' home tomorrow to sign the papers.

Shug hangs up the phone.

SHUG: Come on. Get packed. You get there in time, you can make it to the funeral. Maybe you like him better dead.

Shug laughs.

Outside the store Pants music begins in the underscore.

CELIE: Dear Nettie, I went back home. The house wasn't bad, but the store was a dusty mess. But I fixed it up, and now I'm makin' my pants for everybody that want 'em. I change the cloth, I change the print, I change the waist, I change the pocket. Only thing I can't do is quit makin' em.

Ladies come out of the fitting rooms now, wearing the pants. Celie comments on how good they look, and generally attends to them as...

CELIE: *All I need's a needle and a spool of thread Got about a million patterns in my head All the ladies' legs are gonna love to dance When they in Miss Celie's pants*

GLODENE & ODESSA: *Gabardine, velveteen, satin, or lace Buttons and bows all over the place*

CELIE: *Styles that make you look like a queen*

CHURCH LADIES: *That woman's a wiz with her sewin' machine*

EVERYONE: *Who dat say ~ Who dat say ~ Who dat? ~ Who dat say ~ Who dat say ~ Who dat? ~ Who dat say ~ What you say ~ In Miss Celie's pants! ~ Who dat say ~ Who dat say ~ Who dat? ~ Who dat say ~ Who dat say ~ Who dat? ~ Who dat say ~ What you say ~ In Miss Celie's pants*

SOFIA: *Lookit here ~ Get out my way ~ Sofia's back ~ And I'm here to stay!*

SHUG: *Girl, you swept out the mem'ries ~ Filled this place with joy*

SOFIA: *In this big ol' store*

DORIS: *Got your sewing machines*

DARLENE: *Mirrors shiny clean*

JARENE: *Got some fitting rooms ~ Smell like sweet perfume*

SOFIA: *That man mighta done you wrong*

CELIE: *But look... ~ I said look... ~ Are you lookin'...*

CELIE LOOKS AROUND AT ALL OF THEM AND SINGS TO SHUG.

CELIE: *Look who's wearing the pants now!*

EVERYONE: *Who dat say ~ Who dat say ~ Who dat? ~ Who dat say ~ Who dat say ~ Who dat? ~ Who dat say ~ What you say ~ In Miss Celie's pants!*

THE SIGN APPEARS, WITH HARPO ON A LADDER FINISHING THE PAINTING OF IT. HE IS WEARING A PAIR OF CELIE'S PANTS. MISTER COMES UP TO HIM.

MISTER: What you got on yourself?

HARPO: Pair of Miss Celie's pants. She gon make herself a pile of money doin' this, you know why? This ain't just pants, Pa. Man got this on, he think, things is goin' good for that man. He right where he belong. (A MOMENT) Go on in. Try on a pair. Celie's pants fit anybody.

HARPO GOES OFF DOWN THE ROAD. MISTER FOLLOWS HIM, THEN TURNS AND SEES CELIE LOCKING THE DOOR OF THE STORE FOR THE NIGHT. SHE SEES SOMEONE IN THE STREET. FOR A MOMENT SHE IS ALARMED. SOFIA IS WITH HER. SOFIA CARRIES A SMALL GIRL, HENRIETTA.

CELIE: Who that?

MISTER: It's me...Albert.

CELIE: What you doin' out here?

MISTER: I don't mean to keep you.

SOFIA: Do you want me to stay with you?

CELIE: Thanks.

MISTER: I just wanted to see for myself. Everybody tellin' me what you up to.

CELIE: Come back tomorrow, then. We see what size you are. We getting' more men customers every day.

MISTER: That's all right.

CELIE: Okay, then. Good night.

MISTER TURNS TO SOFIA. THIS IS HIS FIRST ATTEMPT AT THIS, SO IT'S ROUGH, BUT HE'S DETERMINED.

MISTER: Sofia. Maybe you and Celie like to get a soda or something. I could take Henrietta home for you, if you want.

SOFIA AND CELIE ARE BOTH STUNNED, BUT DON'T LET ON. SOFIA WELCOMES THIS MOMENT OF FREEDOM.

SOFIA: Why thank you, Albert. (THEN TO HENRIETTA) Grandpa gon take you home, honey. Go on.

MISTER WALKS OFF WITH HENRIETTA.

CELIE: Well now.

SOFIA: What ton of bricks fell on him?

SOFIA EXITS, AND CELIE AND NETTIE WATCH MISTER WITH HENRIETTA.

CELIE: Dear Nettie, Sofia little girl, Henrietta, turn out she have some kind of blood disease. Yams is sposed to be good for that, but Henrietta hate yams, of course, and she claim she can still taste 'em, throw it out the window, scream and call us names, no matter how we disguise 'em, Mister the only one of us Henrietta don't hate. Last week, he got the idea to hide the yams in some peanut butter. Then he sit with her while she listen to the radio and eat her sandwich. Mister tell Sofia it's time he was good to some little girl.

Scene Six: Night

"Is there any else I can do for you?"

AT HARPO'S HOUSE

HARPO: *I fed the chickens and I chopped the wood ◦ And then I put up the peaches like you said I should ◦ I mended the fences and painted 'em too ◦ Now is there anything I can do for you?*

SOFIA: *I milked twelve heifers by the early morn' ◦ And then I shucked about a hundred ears of corn ◦ I scrubbed all your britches til they look brand new ◦ Now is there anything I can do for you?*

HARPO & SOFIA: *Any little thing you might want me to?*

SOFIA: *I rubbed magnolia petals on my skin*

HARPO: *Mmmm, I cut my toenails and shaved my chin*

SOFIA: *I'll turn out the light*

HARPO: *I'll pour the brew*

HARPO & SOFIA: *Now is there anything else I can do for you? ◦ Any little thing you might want me to? ◦ Any little thing you might want me to?*

HARPO: *Any little thing...*

SOFIA: *Any little thing...*

HARPO: *Any little thing... Yeah ◦ Any little thing...*

SOFIA: *Any little thing...*

HARPO: *Any little thing...*

MISTER ENTERS.

MISTER: HARPO? SOFIA? YOU HOME?

THEY SIGH.

HARPO: WHAT'S GOIN ON, PA?

MISTER: I JUST GOT A LETTER FROM THE MISSIONARIES. IT'S ABOUT NETTIE. YOU MADE THIS PLACE LOOK REAL NICE, SOFIA. MADE A REAL HOME FOR YOU AND HARPO.

HARPO: WHAT'S THE LETTER SAY, PA.

MISTER: LOOK LIKE NETTIE AND THE KIDS HAVIN' SOME TROUBLE GETTIN' HOME. (THEN LOOKING AT THEM) YOU COME BY TOMORROW AND READ IT IF YOU WANT.

MISTER LEAVES.

HARPO & SOFIA: *Now is there anything else I can do for you? ◦ Any little thing you might want me to? ◦ Any little thing you might want me to?*

Scene Seven: Chinese Food

"I'm beautiful, and I'm here"

In the yard—at Shug's house
It's lunchtime. Shug and Celie sit outside eating Chinese food.

CELIE: These wontons so good almost enough to make me want to go to China. I'm gon explode I ate so many.

SHUG: Which fortune you want?

CELIE: This one. (Picks one and opens it) Because you are who you are, your future is gon be happy and bright.

SHUG: That's good.

CELIE (Gives the other one to Shug): Now you. (Shug opens hers, but doesn't read it) Well? What it say?

SHUG: It say I got the hots for a boy of nineteen.

CELIE (Laughs, reaching for it): Let me see.

SHUG: No. I'm tryin' to tell you.

CELIE: Tell me what?

SHUG: I hired a new man to play with the band. I almost didn't cause the only thing he play is the flute. But it turn out that blues flute is the one thing blues music been lacking and the minute I heard Germaine play I knew this for a fact.

CELIE: Germaine.

SHUG: I still love you, Celie...I always will...but I'm getting old. Nobody think I'm good-looking no more, but you. Or so I thought. He's nineteen. A boy. How long can it last? Six months?

CELIE: He a man.

SHUG: I know that. And I know better than to take any of them seriously, but some mens can be a lot of fun.

CELIE: But I love you.

SHUG: All I ask is six months to have my last fling.

CELIE: *But what about trust?*

SHUG: I got to have it, Celie. I'm too weak a woman not to.

CELIE: *What about tenderness?*

SHUG: But if you just give me six months, Celie, I'll try to make our life together what it was.

CELIE: *What about tears when I'm happy?*

SHUG: When it's over, I'll come back to Georgia. Live there if you want.

CELIE: *What about wings when I fall?*

SHUG: My heart hurt so much sayin' this to you.

CELIE: *You said you would be*

SHUG: I love this boy and I'm scared to death...

CELIE: *A story for me*

SHUG: You know this boy gon hurt me twice as much as I'm hurtin' you

CELIE: *That I could believe in forever*

SHUG: ...please just forgive me

CELIE: *So what about, what about*

SHUG: And let me come back when it's over.

CELIE: No. You know I love you and you still do this? No.
(To Shug)
I don't need you to love me
I don't need you to love

Finding her strength

CELIE: *I got... I got...*

I got my sister I can feel her now She may not be here but she still mine And I know she still love me

I got my children I can't hold them now They may not be here but they still mine I hope they know I still love them

Got my house It still keep the cold out Got my chair When my body can't hold out

Got my hands Doin' good like they s'pose to Showin' my heart To the folks that I'm close to

Got my eyes Though they don't see as far now They see more bout how things Really are now...

I'm gonna take a deep breath I'm gonna hold my head up Gonna put my shoulders back And look you straight in the eye I'm gonna flirt with somebody When they walk by I'm gonna sing out... Sing out I believe I have inside of me Everything I need to live a bountiful life With all the love alive in me I'll stand as tall as the tallest tree And I'm thankful for every day that I'm given Both the easy and hard ones I'm livin' But most of all I'm thankful for Knowing who I really am I'm beautiful Yes, I'm beautiful And I'm here

The wisteria blooms.

Scene Eight · Reunion

Celie and Nettie are finally reunited

On Sofia's porch. Mister comes up to the house, still a little out of breath.

MISTER: I stacked all the coke-cola in your wagon, and I filled your big washtub up with ice, so all you have to do is get Harpo to carry it up to the house when you git there.

SOFIA: Whyn't you put all that stuff in your wagon and carry it up yourself?

MISTER: Oh, I'm not goin'. It's just the people Celie likes.

SOFIA: You have to be there. This whole party was your big idea. What you think she's gon do? Tell everybody she hate you? They already know that.

This hurts him. She relents, in her way.

SOFIA: What's the matter with you? All these people know you, Albert.

MISTER: Well. Maybe that's what I'm afraid of.

SOFIA: You different now. You remember that.

MISTER: I know.

SOFIA: So you're comin' to this party. Fraid or not. Is that right?

MISTER: That's right.

SOFIA: And don't be late.

Celie's house. The house looks wonderful now, the trim is painted a cheery color and there are flowers everywhere. It's the 4th of July, 1945. Celie is 50. There are picnic tables set up in the front yard.

A young man comes out of the house, carrying a tool kit.

YOUNG MAN: Your sink workin' just fine now, Miss Celie.

CELIE: How much do I owe you?

YOUNG MAN: Oh don't worry bout it now. I send you a bill. (a moment) How that new bathtub workin' out?

For some reason, this tickles her.

CELIE: It's real nice. You was right about how comfortable it is.

YOUNG MAN: Y'all havin' a picnic.

CELIE: We sure are. I think Sofia and Harpo done invited everybody they ever met. You come too if you want.

YOUNG MAN: I'd like that, if you're sure you got enough.

CELIE: Bring your mama too if she's feeling better. We gon' start about 3.

YOUNG MAN: All right, then. You need anything else done around here, you call me, now. Don't have to be plumbin'.

CELIE: Thank you, Bobby.

He tips his hat, and leaves. Mister appears. He looks great. Cleaned up and looking quite honorable and new.

MISTER: How you doin', Celie?

CELIE: I'm fine.

MISTER: I am, too. I feel like this the first time I ever live on earth as a useful man. I see things. Wonder 'bout stuff.

CELIE: What you wonder about?

MISTER: Why us black? Why us men and women? Why us here in the first place?

CELIE: And what you think.

MISTER: I think us here to wonder. And while us wonder about the big things, us learn the little ones kinda by accident. And the more us wonder, the more us love.

CELIE (a moment): You wanna sit down?

MISTER: I would. Thank you. I brought something to show you. (He hands her a big seashell) I never seen the ocean but I love shells. I ordered this one from a book. You hold this up to yo ear, you hear the ocean. (She puts it up to her ear) You love anything special?

CELIE: Birds, I guess.

MISTER: You used to remind me of a bird, way back when you come to live with me. You was so skinny, the least little thing happen, you look about to fly away.

CELIE: You saw that?

MISTER: I saw it. Just too big a fool to let myself care.

CELIE: Well. Us live through it.

MISTER: I know you hate me for keepin' Nettie's letters.

CELIE: I don't hate you, Albert. I see all these things you're doin' for people now. Buildin' things for the school, helpin' Sofia and Harpo with the kids. (A moment) And the other thing, we both loved Shug. What you love best about her?

MISTER: Her style. She upright and honest. Speak her mind, like Sofia. (A moment) I'm real sorry she left you. I remember how I felt when she left me.

CELIE: It all right. Somebody leave my life, somebody else come, I know that now.

MISTER: Celie. I want you to marry me. For real this time, not just in the flesh but in the spirit too. Will you marry me?

Celie takes a minute.

CELIE: Let's us just be friends.

MISTER: All right, then.

Sofia and Harpo come onstage now, with children and food.

SOFIA: Come on, y'all. Let's get this party started.

HENRIETTA: Why us have to have the 4th of July in July? It's so hot.

Squeak and Grady come on.

MISTER: There's Squeak and Grady. They wasn't sure if they'd get here.

CELIE: And there is Doris, Darlene, and Jarene.

CHURCH LADIES: Hi, Miss Celie! Hi, Mister...Albert!

CELIE: I hope we got enough chicken for all these people.

MISTER: We got enough. I'm sure of it.

Shug appears now.

CELIE: And look at this. Did you know she was coming?

MISTER: I knew she was in town. Sofia say Shug's daddy let her stay at his house this time. I guess she just invited herself to the party.

CELIE: That's all right. I'm glad to see her. She's lookin' good.

MISTER: Real good.

Shug approaches now.

CELIE: How you doin'?

SHUG: I missed you more than I missed my mama.

CELIE: Where's Germaine?

SHUG: Oh. He couldn't come. He had to go to college.

They all laugh.

CELIE (looking off): Now who that comin' in that black car? Everybody I know already in my yard. Who not here, Albert?

Mister and Shug exchange glances. From the distance, a voice is heard.

NETTIE: *Hey, sista, whatcha gon do? ~ Goin' down by the river ~ Gonna play with you*

Celie recognizes Nettie's voice. And responds with her half of their old song. Celie starts to move toward Nettie.

CELIE: *Papa don't like no screamin' round here*

NETTIE & CELIE: *No lip from da woman when he chug dat beer*

A woman with gray hair and two young people come into view.

CELIE: Nettie.

They reach each other and embrace, crying and shaking and are so overcome that they don't even realize anyone else is there.

NETTIE: Celie!

CELIE: Nettie!

Finally, Nettie is able to speak.

NETTIE: Celie, these are your children, Olivia and Adam.

Celie hugs them, then remembers her manners and gestures toward Mister and Shug.

CELIE: This Albert. And this Shug.

NETTIE: Shug come to Ellis Island to speak for us. We love Shug.

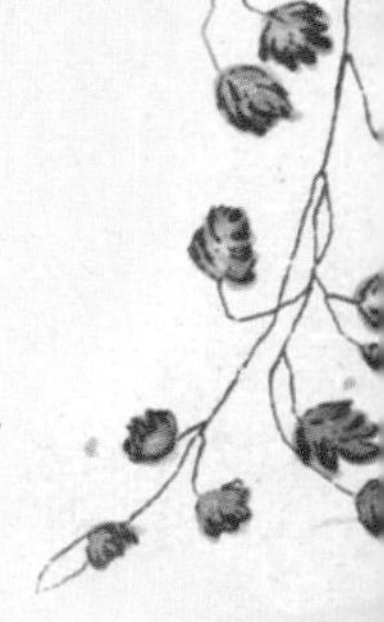

CELIE: EVERYBODY LOVE SHUG. THAT NEVER CHANGE.

SHUG: I LOVE YOU, TOO. BUT IT WAS ALBERT GOT EVERYTHING STRAIGHT WITH THE GOV'MENT SO NETTIE COULD COME HOME.

CELIE LOOKS AT SHUG AND MISTER NOW.

CELIE: YOU TWO DONE THIS FOR ME.

NETTIE: THEY WOULDN'T EVEN LET ME CALL YOU, CELIE.

MISTER: I DIDN'T EVEN TELL HARPO. 'CAUSE HE BOUND TO TELL SOFIA AND SHE TELL EVERYBODY IN TOWN.

CELIE: NETTIE. MY NETTIE HOME.

CELIE: *Dear God, dear stars, dear trees, dear sky* ✣ *Dear peoples, dear everything, dear God*

God is inside me and everything else ✣ *That was or ever will be* ✣ *I came into this world with God* ✣ *And when I finally looked inside I found it*

Just as close as my breath is to me

CELIE LOOKS OUT OVER THE GROUP. SHE IS JOINED BY THE ENSEMBLE.

CELIE/NETTIE/SOFIA: *Rising...*

ADAM/OLIVIA: *Rising...*

SHUG/MISTER/SAMUEL: *Rising...*

CELIE/NETTIE/SOFIA/SHUG/MISTER/ADAM/OLIVIA: *Like the sun* ✣ *It's the hope that sets us free*

CELIE: *Your heart beat* ✣ *Makes my heart beat*

CELIE/NETTIE/SOFIA/SHUG/MISTER/ADAM/OLIVIA: *When we* ✣ *Share love*

FULL COMPANY: *Like a blade of corn* ✣ *Like a honeybee* ✣ *Like a waterfall* ✣ *All a part of me*

Like the color purple ✣ *Where do it come from?* ✣ *Now my eyes are open* ✣ *Look what God has done*

It take a grain of love ✣ *To make a mighty tree* ✣ *Even the smallest voice* ✣ *Can make a harmony*

Like a drop of water ✣ *Keep the river high* ✣ *There are miracles* ✣ *For you and I*

Like a blade of corn ✣ *Like a honeybee* ✣ *Like a waterfall* ✣ *All a part of me*

Like the color purple ✣ *Where do it come from?* ✣ *Now my eyes are open* ✣ *Look what God has done*

CELIE: *I don't think us feel old at all* ✣ *I think this is the youngest us ever felt*

CELIE: *A—*

ENSEMBLE: *A—* ✣ *Men*

CELIE: *Men*

END OF SHOW

Chapter Six

The Impact

Oprah Winfrey becomes the Presenting Producer

SCOTT SANDERS (Lead Producer): I deliberately did not try and get Oprah involved early on. I didn't want to solicit anything from her, and I did not feel that just because she was in the movie, it entitled us to anything. I never, ever would have dreamed of asking her for money. My secret wish was, How can I get her to come to opening night? And if she likes it, will she put our cast on her show? I had hoped, after Quincy Jones became a producer, that he would invite Oprah to the opening. Whether or not she'd come, who knew? And that was where we had left it.

In July 2005, when we got the lease to the Broadway Theatre and knew we were opening in the fall, we had a marketing meeting. I said to our publicist, Carol Fineman, "We'd better think about inviting a long lead editor to the July reading." I had promised my director, Gary Griffin, that the reading would only be for a private audience but I told Carol, "I think we're going to have to invite select members of the press." So I called Quincy and said, "Before we call *Vanity Fair* or *Vogue* or *Essence*, it seems to me that out of respect, we ought to at least let *O* [*The Oprah Magazine*] know that we're doing this."

He said, "Call Gayle King." So I called Gayle, who is the Editor-at-Large of *O* magazine. I have such passion about this project, I can ramble on about *The Color Purple* till the cows come home, and so I started telling her about the show and my journey to bring it to Broadway. We stayed on the phone for about twenty minutes. She said, "I might like to do a story about you doing this." I said, "No, no. I don't want you to do that, but if you're interested in writing about the show, I think you should come see the reading." She asked if she could bring two other editors with her, and I'm thinking, Gary's going to kill me, but said, "Okay, come on."

About three days beforehand, I called her to follow up and she asked, "What time does it start? How long does it last?" I said, "We're running the whole show, so it's about 2-1/2 hours." And she said, "Well, I have a lunch at one o'clock, so I'll probably have to leave at intermission." I'm thinking, "You can't leave at intermission! You have to see the end!" But I'm sort of feeling lucky that she was coming at all, and by that time my sister had told me Gayle King was Oprah's best friend.

When they arrived, I put them on the aisle. At the act break, after Shug and Celie sing their duet "What About Love?" and discover that Nettie's alive, I looked over to see Gayle crying. Then she started typing on her Blackberry. At intermission, she came over to me and said, "I've moved my lunch to two o'clock, and we're going to stay. This is wonderful, and I just e-mailed Oprah and told her that you've done her proud."

I thought, You have her e-mail address in that thing, don't you? At the end, they said they loved it, and then added, "We do want to write a story about this. We need to find a writer, and we'll get back to you." And that was it. We pretty much had raised all the money, and we were starting to build our sets and costumes.

Through the summer, Gayle and I developed an e-mail relationship. When Allee, Brenda, and Stephen wrote a new song, I asked Gayle if she'd want to hear it. She said she'd love to. When the marquee started to go up, I realized that we got the one theater where Gayle could call me and say, "I'm looking out the window and see a big crane putting your sign up."

One day in September, we were talking on the phone, and she asked, "Do you have all your money in place?" I said, "Yes we do." And she said, "Oh, I have someone who might want to invest in the show." I told her we had raised all the money but if she had a friend who wanted to make a small investment, I would try to squeeze them in. Then she said, "Scott, I mean Oprah." I almost fainted.

The next day, I answered my cell phone and it was Oprah Winfrey. She told me that she had heard great things about the show from Gayle and Quincy and asked how she could help. Then she asked if she could invest in the show. I said, "We have all the money. But if you really want to do this, you can help the show with something more important than money. You get your viewers to read Faulkner and the classics, so if you can get people who don't normally go to the theater to come see *The Color Purple*, it will be great for the show and great for all of Broadway." And she said, "Why don't you come see me in Chicago?"

Very quietly, my co-producers Roy Furman and Todd Johnson, along with our senior press and marketing staff, accompanied me to Chicago. Oprah told us how significant *The Color Purple* had been in her life and that she was enthusiastic about the possibility of coming on board as a producer of the Broadway musical. She said it was important to her that she invest her own money in the production. Roy and I found a way to make it work.

I had a big request that I really wanted to ask of her but wasn't sure how she would respond. At what felt like the right moment, I said, "Oprah, we would like you to be more than a producer. Will you agree to let us bill the show as 'Oprah Winfrey Presents *The Color Purple*?'" She said, "Scott, you have been working on this musical for eight years. I worked on *Beloved* for ten years and know what it feels like to dedicate oneself to something for that long. I would never step on your toes that way." I said, "Oprah, my name won't sell two tickets. Your name on the marquee can make a world of difference." So she agreed and then asked, "When can we put the cast on *Oprah*?" This was beyond our wildest dreams.

As Todd and I rode in the taxi on the way to O'Hare Airport, Oprah called me on my cell phone: "Scott, I want to fly to New York tomorrow to see a rehearsal. Let's surprise the cast and hire a camera crew and film the surprise. We can run it on *Oprah* when the cast appears."

The next afternoon, we secretly brought Oprah, along with some of her friends and colleagues, into a private room at The New 42nd Street Studios. I went into the rehearsal room and asked everyone to assemble on the stage. I told them, "I received a call from someone about a week ago who said they had heard a lot of wonderful things about our show. Meet our newest producer." We opened the door and Oprah walked into the room. The emotional response was like a nuclear explosion! The way our cast and creative team already feel about being part of *The Color Purple*, combined with their respect and admiration for Oprah, was so powerful, no one could contain their joy. People were jumping up and down, crying, and cheering. After much hugging and jubilation, Oprah addressed the entire room: "You will find that all things purple are also all things divine. So divine, amazing things happen to you when you are connected to the energy and spirit of this work. There's an energy connected to what Alice first intended. When intention and energy combine and you have

all of that ancestral stuff mixed in there, it's a holy moment for everybody involved. I know you all feel it already and know you will spread that energy to the world, and I feel blessed to be a part of each and every one of you."

After the Premier

LaChanze

Brenda Russell

Virginia Ann Woodruff

Krisha Marcano

MARSHA NORMAN (Book Writer): On opening night, I was knocked out by this feeling of watching myself vanish.

I understood that this was exactly what I was supposed to do on that night: I had finished what I came to do. Now this belongs to the cast, belongs back to Alice, belongs to the world. Belongs to the audience now. It was just this good feeling, like this show is stable and strong and powerful. And I'm free. I was proud. I felt proud and free and invisible. I felt like I had done a thing that I had wanted to do, which was to convey this story on to the Broadway stage with a sense of joy. That's what I wanted. I wanted to make sure that the triumph of this story made it onto the stage. And that it wasn't a wail-y, wail-y, woe is me, art-filled experience. From the very beginning, I thought, This is a piece that belongs to the audience, that belongs to the people whose history it is. It belongs to the people of this country who, whatever race they are, have been involved in this story. This is designed to go straight into the arms of the people who are waiting for it.

SCOTT SANDERS (Lead Producer): The average attendance on Broadway by African Americans in 2005 was 3.8 percent, according to the League of New York Theaters survey. Everyone, including me, thought, Okay, if we can get ten or fifteen percent African American it'll be great. We'll be four or five times the average on Broadway. In fact, *The Color Purple* is getting about a 50/50 black/white audience every performance. So you've got people coming from different places, different worlds, if you will, coming to the Broadway theater. They're sitting down for whatever reason it got them there: it was their favorite book, it was their favorite movie, they hear Oprah Winfrey likes it.

ALICE WALKER: I don't go to see a play by Sophocles just because he's Greek. I love Sophocles and I'm glad he was Greek, but when you get right down to it, when we go to see plays like *Medea* or *Oedipus Rex* or any of those classic amazing plays, it's because they show us something about human beings. And in our country, we are so incredibly mixed that we want to go and see the full spectrum of what we're all doing.

So I'm totally happy at a basic level that there's going to be so much work in the theater for our brilliant performers. We have always had just the most amazing actors, musicians, creative people. And there's going to be lots of work for a long time, I hope. So on that level, as as practical thing, I'm delighted. I'm also delighted that people get to see the beauty of African-American people. There's nothing like it. It's so beautiful. So that's a gift in itself. But beyond that, the letters that I have gotten from people all over the world about the novel and the movie indicate that people relate at the soul level, at the heart level, at the spirit level. And how the people look in terms of their color is really incidental—as I discovered in China and in Japan and in Korea and all over the rest of the world. People relate because it's a story that helps them live.

GARY GRIFFIN (Director): Going into *The Color Purple*, everyone was concerned about the darkness of the story, the potentially depressing story that we were going to tell. That didn't really occur to me in the beginning.

I wasn't prepared for the absolutely celebratory event that happens in the theater every night. It's consistent. It's not like, Oh, we have a good show, bad show. Yeah, our show varies like any show, but every single night, this experience happens. People walk in as a group of individuals, and leave as one group.

I think what's going on is that they're really aware of the human struggle and the human celebration right in front of them. And whatever has gotten them there, they realize all of us in that room are struggling to figure out what we believe in and that we're all overcoming our obstacles, whatever they are. And then, we all love to laugh. And we all love to sing. Those parts of human beings that express themselves through singing and laughter and participation—no matter who we are, there is no barrier and no boundary to that part of being human.

ALICE WALKER: We're on a journey, you know? We're on a journey, and most of it is through ourselves. You know, discovering who we really are and what we would be like and can be like without somebody's foot on our neck.

The Credits and Acknowledgments

TEXT CREDITS: All text by Lise Funderburg, except: © 2006 Oprah Winfrey, 7 (foreword); © 1982 Alice Walker, 12-13 (original handwritten excerpt from the novel); © 2005 Stephen Bray, Brenda Russell, and Allee Willis, 110-177 (music and lyrics of *The Color Purple*); © 2005 Marsha Norman, 110-177 (book of *The Color Purple*).

ILLUSTRATION/ARTWORK: Cover art © 1982, Judith Kazdyn Leeds, courtesy of Harcourt Brace Jovovich, 11 (The Color Purple novel); Poster art © 1985, courtesy of Warner Bros./Amblin Entertainment (original film poster); courtesy of Paul Tazewell, 68 (costume sketches); courtesy of John Lee Beatty, 78-79 (set sketches).

PHOTOGRAPHY CREDITS: All photography by Jennifer S. Altman except: © 2005 Paul Kolnik, 1, 3, 4-5, 6, 31-33, 39, 46-47, 48, 54-55, 56, 58, 94, 104, 110-177; courtesy Alice Walker, 10; courtesy Allee Willis, 18.

PHOTOGRAPHY IDENTIFICATIONS: 1 (from left) Zipporah G. Gatling and Chantylla Johnson; 3 (from left) Renée Elise Goldsberry and LaChanze; 4-5 (top, from left) Elisabeth Withers-Mendes, LaChanze; Brandon Victor Dixon, Felicia P. Fields; Zipporah G. Gatling, LaChanze, Leon G. Thomas III; and LaChanze; (bottom from left) Kingsley Leggs; Brandon Victor Dixon; LaChanze, Renée Elise Goldsberry; Elisabeth Withers-Mendes; Carol Dennis; Kimberly Ann Harris, Maia Nkenge Wilson, and Virginia Ann Woodruff; 6 (from left) Brandon Victor Dixon and Felicia P. Fields; 8 (from left) Zipporah G. Gatling and Chantylla Johnson; 14 (middle left) Todd Johnson and Scott Sanders; (right) Scott Sanders; (bottom) Gary Griffin and Scott Sanders; 15 (from left) Elisabeth Withers-Mendes and LaChanze; 20 (from left) Gary Griffin and Kenita R. Miller; 23 LaChanze; 24 (from top) Kimberly Ann Harris; Virginia Ann Woodruff; (from left) Maia Nkenge Wilson and LaChanze; 27 (from left) Roy Furman, Damian Bazadona, and Trish Santini; 28 (top, from left) Linda Twine, Kenita R. Miller, Allee Willis, LaChanze, and Brenda Russell; (middle, from left) Amy Jacobs, Brenda Russell, Kingsley Leggs, and Brandon Victor Dixon; (bottom, from left) James Brown III, Charles G. LaPointe, and Felicia P. Fields; 29 (top, from left) Kenita R. Miller, Allee Willis, LaChanze, and Brenda Russell; (middle) Kenita R. Miller; (bottom, from left) Nona Lloyd and Gary Griffin; 31 (top, from left) Kingsley Leggs and Lou Myers; (bottom, from left) Krisha Marcano, Brandon Victor Dixon, and Felicia P. Fields; 32 (from left) Zipporah G. Gatling and Kingsley Leggs; 33 (from left) LaChanze and Kingsley Leggs; 39 LaChanze; 40 (from left) Charles Gray, LaChanze, and Renée Elise Goldsberry; 41 LaChanze; 42 Renée Elise Goldsberry and LaChanze; 43 Kimberly Ann Harris, Virginia Ann Woodruff, and Maia Nkenge Wilson; 44 (top, from left) LaChanze, Kingsley Leggs, Grasan Kingsberry, J.C. Montgomery, and Charles Gray; (bottom) James Brown III; 45 LaChanze; 46 (from left) Felicia P. Fields and LaChanze; 47 (top, from left) Krisha Marcano and Brandon Victor Dixon; (bottom) Brandon Victor Dixon; 48 (top, from left) James Brown III, Nathaniel Stampley, J.C. Montgomery, James Harkness, and Grasan Kingsberry; (bottom, from left) Angela Robinson, Bahiyah Sayyed Gaines, LaTrisa A. Coleman, Kimberly Ann Harris, Maia Nkenge Wilson, and Virginia Ann Woodruff; 49 (from left) LaChanze and Elisabeth Withers-Mendes; 50 (top, from left) James Brown III, LaTrisa A. Coleman, Francesca Harper, Elisabeth Withers-Mendes, Carol Dennis, Brandon Victor Dixon, Doug Eskew, and Charles Gray; (bottom, from left) Maia Nkenge Wilson, Virginia Ann Woodruff, Kimberly Ann Harris, Krisha Marcano, and Felicia P. Fields; 51 (from left) LaChanze and Elisabeth Withers-Mendes; 52 (from left) Grasan Kingsberry, James Brown III, James Harkness, and Jamal Story; 53 LaTrisa A. Coleman; 54 Elisabeth Withers-Mendes and LaChanze; 55 (from left) Kimberly Ann Harris, Maia Nkenge Wilson, and Virginia Ann Woodruff; 56 (from left) Brandon Victor Dixon, Elisabeth Withers-Mendes, LaChanze, and Kingsley Leggs; 57 Kingsley Leggs; 58 (from left) Virginia Ann Woodruff, Kimberly Ann Harris, Maia Nkenge Wilson, Carol Dennis, Angela Robinson, LaChanze, and Felicia P. Fields; 59 (top and bottom from left) Brandon Victor Dixon and Felicia P. Fields; 60 LaChanze; 61 (from left) Renée Elise Goldsberry, LaChanze, and Company; 62 (from left) J.C. Montgomery, Stephanie Guiland-Brown, Grasan Kingsberry, Brandon Victor Dixon, Bahayah Sayyed Gaines, Felicia P. Fields, Angela Robinson, LaChanze, James Harkness, Kingsley Leggs, Nathaniel Stampley, Elisabeth Withers-Mendes, and Jamal Story; 64 Jamal Story; 66 (top) Paul Tazewell; (middle, from left) Paul Tazewell and Donna Langman; (bottom, from left) Dora Suarez and David Grevengoed; 69 Felicia P. Fields; 70 (from left) Paul Tazewell, Donna Langman, and Elisabeth Withers-Mendes; 71 (top) Elisabeth Withers-Mendes; (middle, from left) Elisabeth Withers-Mendes, Donna Langman, and Paul Tazewell; (bottom, from left) Donna Langman, Christine Field, Elisabeth Withers-Mendes, and Paul Tazewell; 72 (top, from left) Kimberly Ann Harris, Charles G. LaPointe, and Virginia Ann Woodruff; (bottom, left) Sakie Onozawa; (bottom, right, from left) Paul Tazewell, Bahiyah Sayyed Gaines, Leah Loukas, and Sakie Onozawa; 84 (top, from left) Stephanie Guiland-Brown, James Harkness, Angela Robinson, and Krisha Marcano; (bottom, from left) Grasan Kingsberry, Bahiyah Sayyad Gaines, Jamal Story, Stephanie Guiland-Brown, James Harkness, LaTrisa A. Coleman, Elisabeth Withers-Mendes, LaChanze, Brandon Victor Dixon, and Krisha Marcano; 86 (from left) James Brown III, LaTrisa A. Coleman, Francesca Harper, Grasan Kingsberry, Elisabeth Withers-Mendes, Carol Dennis, Brandon Victor Dixon, Doug Eskew, and Charles Gray; 88 (from left) Stephanie Guiland-Brown and James Harkness; 90 (top, from left) Brandon Victor Dixon, Elisabeth Withers-Mendes, Grasan Kingsberry, LaChanze, Jamal Story, LaTrisa A. Coleman, and James Brown III; (bottom, from left) Gary Griffin, Kingsley Leggs, LaChanze, and Felicia P. Fields; 92 LaChanze; 93 (from left) LaChanze and Elisabeth Withers-Mendes; 94 (all) LaChanze; 96 (from left) Felicia P. Fields and LaChanze; 97 (left, from left) Brandon Victor Dixon and Felicia P. Fields; (left) Felicia P. Fields; 98 (from left) Kingsley Leggs and Leon G. Thomas III; 99 (top, from left) LaChanze, Kingsley Leggs, and Gary Griffin; (bottom, from left) Mia Neal and Kingsley Leggs; 100 (from left) Francesca Harper, Jamal Story, Elisabeth Withers-Mendes, Stephanie Guiland-Brown, and LaTrisa A. Coleman; 101 (left) Elisabeth Withers-Mendes; (right, from left) Elisabeth Withers-Mendes, Gary Griffin, and LaChanze; 102 (from left) Krisha Marcano and Brandon Victor Dixon; 103 (top, from left) Kingsley Leggs, Felicia P. Fields, and Brandon Victor Dixon; (bottom, from left) Brandon Victor Dixon and Felicia P. Fields; 104 (left, from left) Renée Elise Goldsberry and LaChanze; (right, from left) Darlesia Cearcy and LaChanze; 105 (left, from left) Krisha Marcano and Brandon Victor Dixon; (right) Krisha Marcano; 106 (top left, from left) Maryann Lewis-Oberpriller and Kimberly Ann Harris; (top right, from left) Paul Tazewell and Virginia Ann Woodruff; (bottom, from left) Lou Myers and Maia Nkenge Wilson; 108-109 (from left) Kimberly Ann Harris, Maia Nkenge Wilson, Virginia Ann Woodruff, and Company; 110 LaChanze; 112 (from left) Zipporah G. Gatling and Chantylla Johnson; 113 Carol Dennis; 114 (from left) Maia Nkenge Wilson, Virginia Ann Woodruff, and Kimberly Ann Harris; 115 (from left) Nathaniel Stampley, Kimberly Ann Harris, LaTrisa A. Coleman, Doug Eskew, James Brown III, Carol Dennis, Virginia Ann Woodruff, James Harkness, J.C. Montgomery, Jamal Story, and Bahiyah Sayyed Gaines; 117 LaChanze; 118 (from left) LaChanze and Renée Elise Goldsberry; 120 Kingsley Leggs; 122 (from left) LaChanze and Kingsley Leggs; 125 LaChanze; 126 (from left) Brandon Victor Dixon and Felicia P. Fields; 128 (from left) Kingsley Leggs and Brandon Victor Dixon; 130-131 (from left) Kimberly Ann Harris, Virginia Ann Woodruff, Francesca Harper, Carol Dennis, Jeannette I. Bayardelle, Angela Robinson, Felicia P. Fields, and LaChanze; 132 (from left) Krisha Marcano and Brandon Victor Dixon; 134 (from left) Grasan Kingsberry, Nathaniel Stampley, J.C. Montgomery, Kimberly Ann Harris, Stephanie Guiland-Brown, Maia Nkenge Wilson, and Virginia Ann Woodruff; 136-137 (from left) James Harkness, Nathaniel Stampley, Jamal Story, J.C. Montgomery, Grasan Kingsberry, James Brown III, Virginia Ann Woodruff, Kimberly Ann Harris, LaTrisa A. Coleman, and Maia Nkenge Wilson; 139 (from left) LaChanze and Elisabeth Withers-Mendes; 141 (from left) Kingsley Leggs and Lou Myers; 143 (from left) Elisabeth Withers-Mendes and LaChanze; 144 (from left) Elisabeth Withers-Mendes and Kingsley Leggs; 146 (from left) Felicia P. Fields and Nathaniel Stampler; 147 (from left) LaTrisa A. Coleman, Jamal Story, Bahiyah Sayyed Gaines, James Brown III, Elisabeth Withers-Mendes, Francesca Harper, and LaChanze; 148 (from left) Krisha Marcano, Brandon Victor Dixon, and Felicia P. Fields; 149 (from left) LaChanze and Elisabeth Withers-Mendes; 150 (from left) Maia Nkenge Wilson, Kimberly Ann Harris, and Virginia Ann Woodruff; 152 (from left) Zipporah G. Gatling, LaChanze, and Leon G. Thomas III; 153 Nathaniel Stampley; 154-155 Broadway Company; 156 Renée Elise Goldsberry; 158 Felicia P. Fields; 159 LaChanze; 160 (from left) Elisabeth Withers-Mendes, LaChanze, and J.C. Montgomery; 162 (from left) Brandon Victor Dixon, J.C. Montgomery, Felicia P. Fields, Krisha Marcano, Kingsley Leggs; 164 (from left) LaChanze and Kingsley Leggs; 164 (from left) Kingsley Leggs and Brandon Victor Dixon; 167 (from left) Elisabeth Withers-Mendes, LaChanze, and Carol Dennis; 170 (from left) Brandon Victor Dixon and Felicia P. Fields; 171 (from left) Felicia P. Fields and Brandon Victor Dixon; 172 LaChanze; 174 (from left) Renée Elise Goldsberry and LaChanze; 178 (from left) Brandon Victor Dixon, Felicia P. Fields, LaChanze, Kingsley Leggs, Elisabeth Withers-Mendes, and Renée Elise Goldsberry; 181 (from left) Scott Sanders and Roy Furman;182 (top) LaChanze; (middle left) Brenda Russell; (middle right) Virginia Ann Woodruff; (bottom) Krisha Marcano

SPECIAL THANKS TO: Laura Amazzone, Philip Anschutz, Micky Arison, Nick Ashford, Oren Aviv, Jennifer Berger, Jessica Berger, David Binder, Martin Blaustein, Chris Boneau, Susan Bristow, Shanieka D. Brooks, Harold Brown, Andrew Cohen, Dan Cummings, Brian Collins, Patti Connolly, Cem Curosman, Lisa Erspamer, Tom Evered, Debb Foreman, Paul Gongaware, Peter Guber, Lisa Halliday, Matt Hessburg, Zach Hochkeppel, Susan Holland, Mike Issacson, Gordon Jee, Emily King, David Lande, Rocco Landesman, Lori-Nell Lazzeri, Tim Leiweke, Byron Lewis, Bruce Lundvall, John Meglen, Michael Lynch, Gregg Mayday, Jessica J. Miller, Tara Montgomery, Nina Moore, Libby Moore, Desi Moynihan, James L. Nederlander, James M. Nederlander, Jeremy Nussbaum, Randy Phillips, Ellen Rakieten, Bill Rosenfield, Michael Rudell, Gerald Schoenfeld, Harriet Seitler, Jeff Sharp, Valerie Simpson, Michele Singer, Philip J. Smith, Stephanie Snipes, Steven Spielberg, Gloria Steinem, Loreen Williamson, JR Rich, Jay David Saks, Nick Scandalios, Tim Schmidt, Saul Shapiro, Ken Sunshine, David Thomsen, Jack Viertel, Mike Walker, Robert E. Wankel, Daniel Wasser, David Watson, Wendy Weil, Bruce Weinstein, and Eric Woolworth. And to our biggest fan, Gayle King.

Melcher Media would like to thank Kyle Acebo, Jonathan Ambar, Will Balliett, David E. Brown, Cara Di Edwardo, Shaun Dillon, Todd Londagin, Charlie Lora, Lisa Maione, Lauren Nathan, Shoshana Thaler, Lia Ronnen, Jessi Rymill, Alice Siempelkamp, Alex Tart, Anna Wahrman, Betty Wong, and Megan Worman

BIOS:
JENNIFER S. ALTMAN is a photojournalist based in New York City. She began her journey with *The Color Purple* while on a long-term assignment for *Business Week* magazine. Jennifer is also a regular contributor to the *New York Times* and the *Los Angeles Times* and has been published in numerous national and international publications.

LISE FUNDERBURG is an award-winning author, essayist, and critic. She received her undergraduate degree from Reed College in Portland, Oregon, her master's degree in journalism from Columbia University, and is the author of *Black, White, Other: Biracial Americans Talk About Race and Identity*.

PAUL KOLNIK is a well-known New York City-based photographer who specializes in dance and theater.

3+CO. is an award-winning New York design studio owned and operated by three sisters—Merideth Londagin, Jeniffer Cogliantry, and Amy Harte. The group specializes in book design, music packaging, and visual brand management.

This book was produced by MELCHER MEDIA
124 West 13th Street, New York, NY 10011
www.melcher.com

Publisher: Charles Melcher
Associate Publisher: Bonnie Eldon
Editor in Chief: Duncan Bock
Editor: Holly Rothman
Assistant Editor: Lindsey Stanberry
Production Director: Andrea Hirsh

OPRAH WINFREY
SCOTT SANDERS ROY FURMAN QUINCY JONES
CREATIVE BATTERY ANNA FANTACI & CHERYL LACHOWICZ INDEPENDENT PRESENTERS NETWORK
DAVID LOWY STEPHANIE P. McCLELLAND GARY WINNICK JAN KALLISH
NEDERLANDER PRESENTATIONS, INC. BOB & HARVEY WEINSTEIN
ANDREW ASNES & ADAM ZOTOVICH TODD JOHNSON

Present

The Color Purple

A NEW Musical

BASED UPON THE NOVEL WRITTEN BY ALICE WALKER
AND THE WARNER BROS./AMBLIN ENTERTAINMENT MOTION PICTURE

Book by
MARSHA NORMAN

Music and Lyrics by
BRENDA RUSSELL **ALLEE WILLIS** **STEPHEN BRAY**

Starring
LaCHANZE
ELISABETH WITHERS-MENDES FELICIA P. FIELDS
BRANDON VICTOR DIXON DARLESIA CEARCY RENÉE ELISE GOLDSBERRY KRISHA MARCANO
and KINGSLEY LEGGS
with KIMBERLY ANN HARRIS MAIA NKENGE WILSON VIRGINIA ANN WOODRUFF
LOU MYERS CAROL DENNIS
JEANNETTE I. BAYARDELLE JAMES BROWN III ERIC L. CHRISTIAN LaTRISA A. COLEMAN BOBBY DAYE ANIKA ELLIS
DOUG ESKEW BAHIYAH SAYYED GAINES ZIPPORAH G. GATLING CHARLES GRAY GAVIN GREGORY
STEPHANIE GUILAND-BROWN JAMES HARKNESS FRANCESCA HARPER CHANTYLLA JOHNSON GRASAN KINGSBERRY CORINNE McFARLANE KENITA R. MILLER JC MONTGOMERY ANGELA ROBINSON KEMBA SHANNON RICKY SMITH NATHANIEL STAMPLEY
JAMAL STORY and LEON G. THOMAS III

Scenic Design
JOHN LEE BEATTY

Costume Design
PAUL TAZEWELL

Lighting Design
BRIAN MacDEVITT

Sound Design
JON WESTON

Casting
BERNARD TELSEY CASTING

Hair Design
CHARLES G. LaPOINTE

Production Managers
ARTHUR SICCARDI

Production Stage Manager
KRISTEN HARRIS
PATRICK SULLIVAN

Press Agent
CAROL FINEMAN/ BARLOW • HARTMAN

General Management
NINA LANNAN ASSOCIATES/ AMY JACOBS

Advertising
SPOTCO

Marketing
APEL, INC.

Music Director
LINDA TWINE

Dance Music Arrangements
DARYL WATERS

Additional Arrangements
JOSEPH JOUBERT

Music Coordinator
SEYMOUR RED PRESS

Orchestrations
JONATHAN TUNICK

Music Supervisor & Incidental Music Arrangements
KEVIN STITES

Choreographed by
DONALD BYRD

Directed by
GARY GRIFFIN

Company Manager: Kimberly Kelley; Assistant Company Manager: Doug Gaeta; General Press Representative: Barlow • Hartman: Michael Hartman, John Barlow, Leslie Baden; Casting: Bernie Telsey Casting: Bernie Telsey, Will Cantler, David Vaccari, Bethany Knox, Craig Burns, Tiffany Little Canfield, Stephanie Yankwitt, Betsy Sherwood; Associate Director: Nona Lloyd; Assistant to the Choreographer: Ruthlyn Salomons; Stage Manager: Glynn David Turner; Assistant Stage Manager: Neveen Mahmoud; Assistant Stage Manager: Kelly Stillwell; Associate Scenic Designer: Eric L. Renschler; Assistant Scenic Designer: Yoshi Tanokura; Associate Costume Designer: Michael F. Mcaleer; Assistant Costume Designers: Dennis E. Ballard, Christine Field; Assistant to the Costume Designer: Jacob A. Climer; Associate Lighting Designers: Mark T. Simpson, Jennifer M. Schriever; Assistant Lighting Designer: Benjamin Travis; Associate Sound Designer: Jason Strangfeld; Automated Lighting Programmer: David Arch; Fight Director: J. Steven White; Fight Captain: James Brown III; Dialect Coach: Deborah Hecht; Make-Up Design: Angelina Avallone; Production Carpenter: Patrick Sullivan; Head Carpenter/Automation: Charles A. Heulitt III; Assistant Carpenter/Flyman: Brian P. Hutchinson; Assistant Carpenter: Ryan Ensser; Production Electrician: Dan Coey; Production Properties: Noah Pilipski; Production Electrician: James J. Fedigan; Head Electrician: Michael E. Cornell; Assistant Electrician: Gary Marlin; Production Sound: Carin Ford; Production Properties: Michael Pilipski; Head Properties: Noah Pilipski; Wardrobe Supervisor: Deborah A. Cheretun; Assistant Wardrobe Supervisor: James Hall; Star Dresser: Betty A. Gillispie; Dressers: Dora Bonilla, Fred Castner, Christina Dailey, Suzanne Delahunt, Valerie Frith, Maureen George, David Grevengoed, Lizz Hirons, James Hodun, Abbey Rayburn, Jay Woods; Hair Supervisor: Mia Neal; Assistant Hair Supervisor: Sakie Onozawa; Hair Dresser: Leah Loukas; Rehearsal Musicians: Damien A. Bassman, Shelton Becton, Joseph Joubert, Daryl Waters, Buddy Williams; Production Assistant: Angelique Villegas; Child Wrangler: Bridget Walders; Advertising: Spotco/Drew Hodges, Jim Edwards, Tom Greenwald, Tom Mccann, Lauren Hunter, John Lanasa, and Kim Smarsh; Marketing & Sponsorship: Apel, Inc./David Sass, Harry Spero, Mathew Farkash, Jessica Stock; Outreach Marketing: Sandie Smith; Website: Design & Online; Marketing Strategy: Situation Marketing LLC/Damian Bazadona, Ian Bennett, Sara Fitzpatrick; Legal Counsel: M. Graham Coleman, Esq. and Robert J. Driscoll, Esq./Davis Wright Tremaine LLP.; General Management Associate: Katherine McNamee; Production Photographers: Joan Marcus and Paul Kolnik; Study Guide: Camp Broadway; Merchandising: Dewynters/James Decker; Assistant to Ms. Norman: Brian Tucker; Assistant to Mr. Bray, Ms. Russell & Ms. Willis: Richard Todd Loyd; Assistant To Mr. Sanders: Scott Pyne; Assistant To Mr. Furman: Eileen Williams; Assistant To Mr. MacDevitt: Jessica Burgess; Music Dept. Assistant: Nathan Kelly

Alliance Theatre Staff
Artistic Director: Susan V. Booth
Managing Director: Thomas Pechar
Associate Artistic Director: Kent Gash
General Manager: Max Leventhal
Director of Marketing: Virginia Vann
Director of Finance: Sallie Lawrence
Director of Development: Andrea Dillenburg
Production Manager: Rixon Hammond